Frame-by-Frame Stop Motion

T0138730

THE GUIDE TO NON-PUPPET PHOTOGRAPHIC ANIMATION TECHNIQUES

Frame-by-Frame Stop Motion

THE GUIDE TO NON-PUPPET PHOTOGRAPHIC ANIMATION TECHNIQUES

SECOND EDITION

Tom Gasek

CRC Press
Taylor & Francis Group
Boca Raton London New York

CRC Press is an imprint of the
Taylor & Francis Group, an **informa** business

A FOCAL PRESS BOOK

CRC Press
Taylor & Francis Group
6000 Broken Sound Parkway NW, Suite 300
Boca Raton, FL 33487-2742

International Standard Book Number-13: 978-1-4987-8061-2 (Paperback)
                                      978-1-1386-2888-5 (Hardback)

Library of Congress Cataloging-in-Publication Data

Names: Gasek, Tom, author.
Title: Frame-by-frame stop motion : the guide to non-traditional animation techniques / Tom Gasek.
Description: Second edition. | Boca Raton : CRC Press, 2017.
Identifiers: LCCN 2016041663 | ISBN 9781498780612 (pbk. : alk. paper)
Subjects: LCSH: Animation (Cinematography) | Stop-motion animation films.
Classification: LCC TR897.5 .G38 2017 | DDC 777/.7--dc23
LC record available at https://lccn.loc.gov/2016041663

**Visit the Taylor & Francis Web site at
http://www.taylorandfrancis.com**

**and the CRC Press Web site at
http://www.crcpress.com**

Printed and bound in the United States of America by Sheridan

Dedication

I would like to dedicate this edition to all the filmmakers who dug in and tried these techniques with the guide of *Frame-by-Frame Stop Motion*. A lot of this kind of animation can be logical and intuitive, but knowing where to start can be challenging. If you are in film school, then you have a "leg up." It certainly is not necessary to have this kind of advantage, as is evident by the many online Lego animations that are out there on the web. There is no reason to reinvent the wheel, so this book is designed to act as a map to this world, with no limitations on where you can go. Having a crew and/or friends is very helpful for exchanging ideas and experiences and sharing the practical responsibilities of filmmaking. When I started the first edition of this book, I turned to a couple of my old colleagues and friends, Bryan Papciak and Jeff Sias, who I worked with in stop motion more than 20 years ago in Boston. We share a love for this kind of work, which has allowed each of us to go deeper into stop motion in preproduction, production, and post-production. It is hard and challenging work—if you don't love some aspect of it, whether it be the process, the animated results, or the response of an appreciative audience, then you shouldn't practice these techniques. However, since Bryan, Jeff, and I share this love and interest, it makes it easy to communicate and share our knowledge with each other and others. Once again, I leaned on Bryan to help review my new additions and I am most thankful for his insights. As I continue to observe the growing number of artists using these techniques, I have been very impressed with the range and variety of approaches. Many artists have extended these techniques with postproduction enhancements as I have done in my own filmmaking. Yet, this direction is not necessary for a successful film. So I want to dedicate this second edition to the mature artists and practitioners of these photographic animation techniques along with the countless neophytes stepping into this world. In the end, it is all about ideas, experiences, imagination, and communication that can come in any form.

Contents

Chapter 1 touches on the meaning of alternative stop-motion
techniques. This chapter highlights key people in history
and their different approaches to stop motion. It addresses
the possibilities of applying these approaches to animation.

Chapter 2 sets up the study of the frame-by-frame stop-motion
approach by addressing preproduction requirements. It discusses
the importance of using this approach to serve an idea and
the hardware and software needed to execute these techniques.

Chapter 3 digs into how pixilation works and the best way to take advantage of it. Some basic but important principles of animation that apply to pixilation are reviewed.

Chapter 4 explores the well-established technique of time lapse, which has little written about it. Technical, conceptual, and practical issues are discussed in this chapter, with an explanation of the best way to get effective results. Cameras, equipment, formulas, and software are revealed.

Chapter 5 reviews many filmmaking techniques, principles, and concepts that apply to live-action and stop-motion puppet animation but are geared toward alternative stop-motion techniques. There are many adjustments to these approaches to cinematography that need to be altered in order to get the most from pixilation, time lapse, and downshooting.

Chapter 6 studies the subject in front of the camera. Certain materials and uses of materials work better than others for specific alternative animation approaches. This chapter also discusses the role of the animator or actor as the animated object.

Chapter 7 covers the third general area of alternative stop-motion techniques: downshooting. This chapter highlights the most popular techniques and suggests additional ones. This chapter includes diagrams and explanations for making your own stand and getting the most from it.

Chapter 8 suggests various ways to add drama and interest to your non-puppet stop-motion films. These approaches include animation principles, composition, lenses, and performance among other references and tips.

Chapter 9 brings in the element of sound and music and discusses their important relationship to picture. This is similar to other techniques in filmmaking, but specific exercises are suggested. This chapter describes frame-by-frame matching of picture and sound and includes information about breaking down music for animation.

Chapter 10 provides a more technical explanation of
how to expand upon footage that has been shot with
alternative forms of stop motion. This chapter covers
postproduction techniques and software used in this area.

Chapter 11 discusses the editing process in relationship
to these alternative techniques. Preproduction and
postproduction editing can make all the difference in the
refinement of a film. This chapter discusses the use of editing
software and the various details and principles involved.

Chapter 12 concludes the book with a discussion of how
filmmakers can capitalize on their alternative frame-by-frame
work. Websites, documenting the process, and festivals are
a few of the topics covered in this important final chapter.

Acknowledgments

The critical elements to this text are the many contemporary artists and film-makers who contributed comments and images to this study of alternative stop-motion photographic techniques. These include Terry Gilliam, Jan Svankmajer, PES, Blu, William Kentridge, Dave Borthwick, Nick Upton, Dave Sproxton, Heather Wright and Aardman Animations, Jan Kounen, Carolyn Leaf, Evan Spiridellis, Jim Blashfield, Joan Gratz, Joanna Priestley, Ken Murphy, Miki Cash, Eric Hanson, Tom Lowe, Yuval and Merav Nathan, Chris Church, Geoff Tompkinson, Keith Loutit, Victoria Mather, Julian Tryba, Corrie Parks, Juan Pablo Zaramella, Bryan Papciak, Daniel Sousa, Eugene Mamut, Joe Lewis, Jamie and Dyami Caliri, Adam Fisher, Monica Garrison, J.P. Crangle, The National Film Board of Canada, Lindsay Berkebile, Jordan Greenhalgh, Jason McLagan, Rachel Fisher, Marlee Coulter, Stevie Ward, Knhik Haefner, Linda Grossman, and the School of Film and Animation at the Rochester Institute of Technology. There are many more artists and filmmakers who are practicing these techniques than I was able to cite or interview. These frame-by-frame techniques are as varied as the artists who practice them, and I was only able to touch on a few approaches. I did try to incorporate principles and practices that are common to most of these techniques, but I am sure that I have left out a few. My aim is to open up the door a bit wider to hand-made photographic animation approaches. These approaches have been evolving as technology has continued to expand, and this makes these techniques as viable as ever. All you have to do is scan the web and see what is out there, and suddenly you will realize that this is a vast and potentially exciting area of filmmaking. The old saying "what is old is new" applies to this book, but again technology has made these approaches to single-frame photographic filmmaking much more accessible. I hope many new filmmakers from all backgrounds are able to explore this area of animation.

This book can serve as a guide. So I acknowledge all the new filmmakers and established filmmakers who want to expand their means of expression through frame-by-frame photographic animation.

Drawn illustrations by Brian Larson.

Photographic illustrations by Tom Gasek and artists cited in each chapter.

Author

Tom Gasek has more than 30 years of award-winning professional stop-motion animation experience as an animator and director. He has worked with directors Will Vinton, Art Clokey, and Henry Selick. At Aardman Animations, he contributed animation to Nick Park's Wallace and Gromit short film *The Wrong Trousers* and the Peter Lord/Nick Park feature film *Chicken Run*. Tom codirected and animated the *Inside-Out Boy* for Nickelodeon, which is a part of the permanent collection at the Museum of Modern Art in New York. Tom maintained two small stop-motion studios, Sculptoons in San Francisco and OOH, Inc., in Massachusetts. Most recently, Tom contributed animation to Aardman's *Creature Comforts America*, Sony Bravia's *Play-Doh*, Laika Entertainment's *Coraline*, and a series of Amazon Prime spots for Hornet Inc. 2016, and he continues to direct and animate commercials and independent films. In the past several years, Tom has produced, directed, and animated two award-winning short independent stop-motion films, *Off-Line* and *Ain't No Fish*. This book is the second edition of his 2011 book *Frame-by-Frame Stop Motion* (Focal Press), which is the only complete resource of its kind on photographic non-puppet stop-motion techniques. He has trained animators at Se-ma-for Studios in Lodz, Poland, and given workshops, based on his book, in Lima, Peru (on a Fulbright grant), at the New Orleans International Children's Film Festival, and the National Museum of Play in Rochester, New York. Tom teaches stop-motion animation, acting for animation, and the business of animation in the School of Film and Animation at Rochester Institute of Technology (RIT). His work can be viewed at www.tdgasek.com as well as on https://vimeo.com/user3424683.

Introduction

A Second Look

I was taken by surprise when Focal/CRC Press contacted me and asked if I would consider a second edition of the book *Frame-By-Frame Stop Motion*. The first thing I did was to go back and review the original book and see if there were things that were missing. I found the original manuscript quite thorough but considered a few things I and others have been doing with these non-puppet stop-motion techniques. Naturally, I always have an eye to the Internet and other venues to see what various artists have been doing with these approaches, and soon some new ideas started to appear. My original premise that non-animators from live-action production and photography would continue to have an interest in this area continues to ring true. In the class I created, based around these techniques, I keep finding a larger number of young artists from various disciplines who like these techniques because they are accessible and they utilize equipment that is familiar. Ultimately, the DSLR camera is one of the core pieces of equipment utilized in stop motion. Cameras of all kinds are combined with capture software, editing programs, and often composite programs to define this look. I actually consider stop motion to be a "photograph art" or "photo animation." By "non-puppet" I mean animated objects that were not made to be animated. They already exist and have been manufactured for something else. This includes furniture, vegetables, sand, photographs, buttons, pool balls, automobiles, and even humans! The list is endless. Many of these non-puppet techniques come very close to puppet or prefabricated model approaches. The bonding elements are the principles of animation.

We continue to love photographic images, which give a nice contrast to computer-generated images. We know the world around us and how it looks, but starting to manipulate that world through time lapse and dynamic frame-by-frame animation of objects, people, or places makes our "real" world a little different. It allows us to view the world from another perspective. The amazing world of artists like Keith Loutit and Geoff Tompkinson reveal photographic images that show great imagination by the manipulation of time-lapse photography. We examined Ken Murphy's *A History of the Sky* time lapse off the roof of the Exploratorium in San Francisco in the first edition, but many artists are expanding this one area of non-puppet frame-by-frame photographic stop-motion animation. Other artists are exploring pixilation of objects and people, and some artists are screening their work in art galleries, on the Internet, in commercial venues, and independent films. I wanted to explore this continued development in this second edition by highlighting several artist-practitioners in the "PRO-file" sections.

After so many years as a commercial puppet stop-motion animator with scores of commercials, TV series work (*Pee-wee's Playhouse*), feature work (*Chicken Run* and *Coraline*), and independent film work (*The Wrong Trousers* and my own *Off-Line* and *Ain't No Fish*), I decided to try a series of pixilated films myself. Performance has always been a big part of my puppet work, and crafting characters makes the animation interesting and challenging. I love this work, and trying to apply this to some pixilated films created some ideas. I once led an independent study with a former student and now professional animator, Lindsay Berkebile, based on acting for pixilation. Applying acting principles to pixilation became a new obstacle for us during this study, but we learned a lot about the most effective expressions and stylization that suits pixilation. How do you elicit emotion from a vibrating, active human or object? I decided to produce a short series of pixilated self-portraits, which would allow me to not only animate but also to be the animated subject. I am applying acting principles along with animation principles in my performances and experiment with subjects that are reflective of my life. Walking, trains, drums, and water are subjects I am tackling that have meaning in my life and will allow me to make this series and experiment with photographic pixilated animation in short films. Since I am halfway through this project, I can share my thoughts and experiences in this second edition book, which will hopefully add depth to the original subject.

Since the first edition of this book, I have created and led workshops for children in New Orleans, for advanced graduate students at Fabrica in Treviso, Italy, and for media professionals in Lima, Peru. There continues to be excitement at all levels about how movement works and the various emotions it can elicit. We are talking about animation, which is my love. I believe that it is movement that draws out emotion and empathy. What is the body rhythm of an individual, what are the gestures that give the director what she or he is looking for, and how can you stylize movement so it has more punch and effect? These are the areas that this second edition will cover in conjunction with these non-puppet stop-motion photographic animation techniques. So let's dive in and see what various artists are creating and what possibilities there are for you, no matter what background or skills you bring to this discipline.

What Are the Possibilities?

Norman McLaren from the NFBC. (Courtesy of Evelyn Lambart, National Film Board of Canada, 1952.)

Creating Magic
Silent Films and Beyond
Stop Motion and Its Various Faces

Creating Magic

The history of these animation art forms has not changed since the first edition of this book. History is written in stone, depending a little on the perspective from which it is told, but the present and the future are always organic and fluid. It does not make sense to try to parse out individuals and examples of work that were not as significant as the examples cited in the previous volume, but there have been some significant iterations of these techniques in the last 5 years. I will be citing several of these new and individual approaches to demonstrate the infinite possibilities that continue to unfold in photographic frame-by-frame non-puppet stop motion.

Humans are social creatures that have an innate need to share experiences and stories. Ever since humankind started communicating, stories that are real and unreal have been shared around the communal circle. The tribe was gathered together and a tale was told that revealed information, lessons, provocative thought, and emotional empathy. Often the more fantastic the story the more entranced the audience became and the stronger the message. This might have been the job of the shaman or chief, but soon everyone had stories and experiences to relate. Eventually stories became enhanced from the oral tradition through props and other means of visual storytelling. In just over the last hundred years, filmmaking has become a powerful vehicle to relate stories and to capture an audience's imagination. Sight and sound are our most primal senses and filmmaking taps into these receptors. Soon after its introduction, filmmaking started to expand its repertoire and the "fantastic" became a possibility in storytelling.

Single-frame filmmaking has been around as long as film itself. The idea of fooling or tricking the eye has always been fascinating to people and the manipulation of live-action filming was the origin of this technique. Imagine the early days of filmmaking when audiences were seeing projected images on a screen, images that appeared to be alive and real for the first time. That was magic in itself. When filmmakers became a bit more sophisticated by stopping the camera in midshoot, removing an object from in front of the camera, and then continuing to film, the results were genuinely magic. As film started to mature, artists and practitioners began to see the endless possibilities that this new medium offered. This stopping the motion of filming and adjusting images, cameras, and events was the predecessor to special effects and animation.

We are talking about stop-motion photography, which has evolved into many variations. The most common form of stop motion that is recognized today is model or puppet stop motion. This is when figurative models are fabricated and animated frame by frame to create a narrative or experimental approach. Examples of this form are seen in films and on television. Feature films like Jiri Trnka's *A Midsummer Night's Dream*, Nick Park and Peter Lord's *Chicken Run*, and *Coraline*, directed by Henry Selick, all exemplify this popular approach to figurative puppet stop motion. Television has also laid claim to this form of animation with popular programs like *Pingu*, *Gumby*, the Rankin/Bass Christmas special *Rudolph the Red-Nosed Reindeer*, and *Robot Chicken*. These, among other titles in this genre, are well loved and are considered more in the realm of traditional stop-motion puppet animation. *Robot Chicken*, created by Seth Green and Matthew Senreich, occasionally uses existing objects or models, but the fabricators adapt these objects or models to work for animation so they are a crossbreed of puppet and non-puppet/object animation. The work of PES is also a great example of an artist who crosses the gap between puppet and non-puppet stop-motion work.

The nontraditional or alternative use of stop motion utilizes people, objects, various materials like sand, clay, and paper, and often a mixture of these and other elements as the objects to be animated. The most common of the non-traditional alternative stop-motion techniques is known as "pixilation." This term is attributed to the Canadian animator Grant Munro, who worked at the National Film Board of Canada with Norman McLaren in the 1940s, 1950s, and 1960s. Both McLaren and Munro were major contributors to this art form. In pixilation, usually a person is animated like a puppet or model. There is a limited amount of registration in this approach to stop motion so the result is a rather kinetic, bewitched, fragmentary movement that appears pixilated or broken up. It has nothing to do with the modern-day term related to low-resolution digital images. Time-lapse photography and "downshooting" (animation on a custom animation stand), also known as "multiplane animation," are two other forms of nontraditional alternative stop-motion photographic animation. We will explore each of these approaches and more in the following chapters.

Silent Films and Beyond

This interest in the manipulation of filming and single-frame adjustment started as soon as film arrived on the scene in the late nineteenth and early twentieth centuries. The Lumière brothers are considered to have been the first to successfully shoot and project films for audiences (Figure 1.1).

Figure 1.1

Auguste and Louis Lumière, circa 1895. (From Auguste and Louis Lumière, https://en.wikipedia.org/wiki/Auguste_and_Louis_Lumi%C3%A8re.)

Their work was amazing to the French and, ultimately, international audiences of the late 1890s. Everyday scenes of that era are well recorded and documented in the factories and streets of Lyon, France. Once audiences became accustomed to the novelty of moving images, then the experimentation began. There were several artists who took the filmmaking technique much farther than Auguste and Louis Lumière, but the most significant artist was Georges Melies (Figure 1.2).

The Parisian-born Melies was often referred to as the "cinemagician." His work with film was influenced by his experience as a stage magician. Melies learned how to use multiple exposures, dissolves, time-lapse photography, editing techniques, and substitution photography where the camera was stopped and the subject was changed to create a magical effect. These silent films created in the late nineteenth and early twentieth century were like magic shows that featured special effects. This kind of filmmaking was the precursor to several different branches in the tree of stop motion, including modern-day special effects, puppet or model stop motion, and pixilation and its various forms. Melies' *The Conjuror*, filmed in 1899, is a clear example of the relationship that he made between magic and his filmmaking (Figure 1.3).

In the film, he covers a woman with a cloth and pulls it off, revealing that the woman has disappeared and reappeared on an adjacent table. He then, through what appears to be magic, continuously switches positions with the woman using smoke and confetti to enhance the effect. This is most likely attained by editing the film and reenacting the action with different elements. The camera must be locked down in one position in order for this to work. The continuous movement of the actors helps create a smooth transition from one person or object to the next. The editing process was the first technique used in the manipulation of imagery, but before too long frame-by-frame manipulations shot in the camera became the most effective way to have ultimate control over the film's outcome.

Another French contributor to stop motion and pixilation was Emil Cohl. His 1911 film *Jobard ne peut pas voir les femmes travailler* (Sucker Cannot See the Women Working) utilized real people and is one of the earliest pixilated films known. Unfortunately, many of Cohl's films have been lost due to fire and neglect.

Figure 1.2

Georges Melies, circa 1890. (From Georges Méliès, https://en.wikipedia.org/wiki/Georges_M%C3%A9li%C3%A8s.)

Figure 1.3

The Conjuror, 1899. (From *The Conjuror*, 1899, https://www.youtube.com/watch?v=zs5BBaNJ6mg.)

1. What Are the Possibilities?

Figure 1.4

Black Maria studio, circa 1893. (Courtesy of the Black Maria Film Festival, Jersey City, NJ.)

The Edison Company, founded by Thomas Edison, created some of the first motion pictures in the United States in his infamous Black Maria studio in West Orange, New Jersey, in 1893 (Figure 1.4).

Similar to the Lumière brothers, Edison's first films reflected everyday life and activities. Edison also attracted audiences and talent like the first established American stop-motion animators, James Blackton and Willis O'Brien. Both artists favored model or puppet animation. O'Brien produced special effects films like the 1915 *The Dinosaur and the Missing Link: A Prehistoric Tragedy* and the eventual 1933 *King Kong*. Artists were moving away from the obvious tricks of dissolves, position replacements, and editing techniques to techniques that were the beginnings of special effects and model animation. Pixilation took a back seat. Even artists like Charley Bowers favored models, as was illustrated in his 1930 film *It's a Bird*, where Bowers has a bird eating metal materials and a car appears to be destroyed frame by frame as the film is run in reverse. This gives the appearance of the car assembling itself totally unassisted (Figure 1.5).

It is worth noting the Russian-born Polish animator Ladislas Starevich, who in 1910 was creating documentary films for the Museum of Natural History in Kovno, Lithuania. The final film in a series was focused on a fight between two stag beetles. Because these beetles would become dormant when the movie lights were on, Starevich decided to use dead beetles and, in place of their legs, to attach wire to their thoraxes with sealing wax. This innovative thinking started a whole new approach to stop motion, which ultimately led to much more developed model animation.

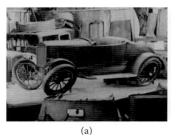

(a)   (b)

Figure 1.5

(a) Car assemblage from *It's a Bird* by (b) Charley Bowers, circa 1935. ((a) From YouTube, *It's A Bird* (1930), https://www.youtube.com/watch?v=Z4I15-7L0ss; (b) from from Wikipedia, Charles_Bowers, https://en.wikipedia.org/wiki/Charles_Bowers#/media/File:Charley_Bowers.jpg.)

In 1929, Russian director Dziga Vertov created a silent documentary film called *Man with a Movie Camera*. In this film, Vertov documents the lives of urban citizens in Odessa. The film, which was edited by his wife and partner, Elizaveta Svilova, features many of the techniques that we will discover in the following chapters. Not only does Vertov use freeze frames, double exposures, reverse playback, fast and slow motion, dynamic camera angles, and editing techniques, but he also uses stop-motion approaches to reveal a rather frenetic and modern existence. It is worth viewing this wonderful documentary film for its historical and aesthetic approach.

Stop Motion and Its Various Faces

It wasn't until 1952 that the technique of pixilation became utilized in a film that struck an international chord. It was Norman McLaren's Academy Award–winning *Neighbours*, which featured Grant Monroe, mentioned earlier as the person who coined the term "pixilation" that put this technique back in the public eye (Figure 1.6).

McLaren's use of animated people and objects, dramatic action, and art direction made the technique perfect for this film. The battle between neighbours, conducted in an extremely territorial fashion, has great humor but also a dark tone that delivers a message in an effective manner. Pixilation continued to grow after McLaren's continued use of this technique. One of the most notable and inspirational masters of this technique is the Czech surrealist Jan Svankmajer. Although Svankmajer used puppets on occasion, he also used everything from humans to meat to household furniture as animated objects. His concentration on textural imagery and suggestive conceptual filmmaking made him stand out from all other filmmakers. His 1971 film *Jabberwocky*, based on a poem by Lewis Carroll, features a cabinet running through a forest, dancing clothes, maggot-ridden apples, distraught dolls, and flipping puzzle parts (Figure 1.7).

Figure 1.6

Neighbours by Norman McLaren (1952). (Courtesy of National Film Board of Canada, Montreal, Quebec, Canada. Photo credit: Evelyn Lambert.)

Figure 1.7

Jabberwocky cabinet in woods, Jan Svankmajer (1971). (Courtesy of Jan Svankmajer. Photos © Athanor Ltd Film Production Company, Jaromir Kallista and Jan Svankmajer.)

Stop Motion and Its Various Faces

Figure 1.8

Still from *Gisele Kerozene* by Jan Kounen. (Courtesy of Tawak Pictures, Paris, France, © 1989.)

Although Svankmajer uses puppets, he mixes his animated subject matter so wildly that the photographic, textural, fast-paced editing leaves the audience feeling rather assaulted. Animators like the American Mike Jittlov, with his pixilated 1979 film *The Wizard of Speed and Time*, and French-born Jan Kounen continued using the pixilation technique with obvious influence from their predecessor, Norman McLaren. In Kounen's 1989 *Gisele Kerozene*, the use of dramatic facial makeup and costuming remind us of the faces of McLaren's two neighbours as they start to get deeply into their fight (Figure 1.8).

Kounen even uses classic Warner Brothers cartoon animated motion when his animated people smash into walls. Wide-angle lenses are used for exaggerated effect. Pixilation is starting to mature. The technique is no longer just a humorous or gimmicky style but a technique that can be chosen as a cinematic device. Dave Borthwick's 1995 feature film *The Secret Adventures of Tom Thumb* is a fascinating and dark film that expands the pixilation technique with a very distinctive story. Nick Upton is Tom Thumb's father and he plays this role with a McLaren sense of exaggeration. This English actor holds his jaw out to maintain a particular look and refines the element of acting associated with this physically challenging technique. Controlling involuntary facial and bodily actions requires extreme control and awareness, often for hours and hours of shooting time and Upton does this quite well (Figure 1.9).

Finally, it is worth noting the Peter Gabriel music video *Sledgehammer*. This 1986 groundbreaking animated short was produced by Limelight London and directed by Stephen R. Johnson, featuring the work of Aardman Animations and the Brothers Quay. It mixed mediums and featured Peter Gabriel lip-syncing or mimicking the words to this wonderful piece of music frame by frame and interacting with everything from fish to fruit to people to clothes and the woodwork itself. Most of these examples, including *Sledgehammer*, were produced and shot directly in the camera. There were very few postproduction effects added, which points out the clever and innovative approach these filmmakers used. This direct application of effects shows a resourcefulness that offers a unique look and cost-saving production (Figure 1.10).

Pixilation has become quite popular in film and animation programs across the country and the world. The technique is relatively inexpensive to produce

Figure 1.9

Still from *The Secret Adventure of Tom Thumb*, Bolex Brothers, 1993 (Nick Upton with exaggerated face). Photo by Nick Spollin. (Courtesy of Dave Borthwick. © Bolex Brothers, 1989.)

Figure 1.10

Peter Gabriel acting in the *Sledgehammer* video, Limelight, 1986. (Courtesy of Real World Music Ltd/Peter Gabriel Ltd/Real World Productions Ltd. © Real World Productions Ltd and Peter Gabriel Limited.)

and very direct in terms of the outcome. It does require proper planning, like any effective use of animation, but you can get fast results and learn a lot of animation techniques by just grabbing a camera, stop-motion animation software, and objects or friends. On a professional level there is more pixilation and mixed media out in the mainstream of our society than ever before. One example is *Her Morning Elegance*, directed and produced by Yuval and Merav Nathan, an Israeli couple who work in various animated techniques and genres. This music video is shot with a static camera mounted directly above a bed. A woman, man, and objects are shot frame by frame in a controlled environment in a very stylized manner, depicting walking, movement in a subway, and swimming underwater all on top of the bed. The static background sets off the animated motion of the people, cloth, and various objects in a very satisfying manner (Figure 1.11).

Two other extensions of pixilation are seen in the work of Blu and PES. Each artist uses pixilation but in very different ways. Blu works outdoors painting walls and animating figures and objects on cityscapes. His camera work is unregistered and quite active, but the dominant drawn figures in the frame maintain the focus of each shot, as in his 2008 film *Muto* and his 2010 film *Big Bang Big Boom*. PES works with objects in a very controlled manner, creating events and environments out of everyday objects, as in his 2008 film *Western Spaghetti*. In this animated short the simple use of candy corn vibrating frame by frame on a stove top mimicking gas-fueled flames sets the style that unfolds in this cooking experience. PES animated stuffed chairs having sex on a roof in New York City in his 2001 film *Roof Sex* (Figure 1.12).

Figure 1.11

Still from *Her Morning Elegance*, Yuval and Merav Nathan. Photograph by Eval Landesman. (Courtesy of Oren Lavie © 2009.)

Figure 1.12

Chairs on a roof in *Roof Sex*. (Courtesy of PES Productions LLC, Wilmington, DE, © 2001.)

Time-lapse photography is a form of frame-by-frame stop motion that is shot in a controlled and consistent manner. The effect of time lapse is that it speeds up time and events so that the viewer can study an event from a different point of view. This perspective and different temporal perception can give us a more expanded understanding of our world and ourselves. One of the most common uses of this technique is the blossoming of a flower sped up to ten or more times the actual event. Anyone can see an hour of real time go by in just one second. There is so much more that can be achieved with this approach to stop-frame photography. Not only can events be recorded at an accelerated rate, but animators can also use this technique to pixilate objects and people. It is critical that the time-lapse camera have an "intervalometer" or timer associated with the camera so the shutter can expose the film or digital image sensor at an even rate. The even exposure rate or shooting interval of the camera reveals the natural rate or evolution of an event in nature sped up and compressed into a short viewing time.

Once again, George Melies was a pioneer in this area. His continued experimentation with film found him exploring time lapse as is seen in the 1897 film *Carrefour de l'Opera* (Crossroads of the Opera). Other early uses of time lapse were associated with science. Biology and various phenomena of nature became the prime focus for this technique. Time lapse has the benefit of speeding up slow action and motions, giving the viewers a better understanding of how nature works. The Russian-American Roman Vishniac used it in the early twentieth century; his interest in nature included microscopic photography and the movement of living creatures. The work of John Ott in the 1930s, 1940s, and 1950s became a technique landmark. Ott, an American banker by trade, was fascinated with the growth of flowers and how nature and light affected them. He cobbled together enough photography equipment controlled by an intervalometer and put his lens on various plants in his own greenhouse. His expanded knowledge of how plants grow and are affected by the environment led him deeper into this technique of stop-frame photography. He created an early motion-control machine that moved the camera increment by increment, frame by frame as the camera captured a plant's progress over a long period of time. This movement of the camera from position A to B added a poetic element to the more scientific locked camera positions (Figure 1.13).

This inspired many filmmakers for years to come, including the rich and refined time-lapse photography of the British filmmaker David Attenborough, as illustrated in his 1995 film *The Private Life of Plants*. There are many sequences in this film of plant flytraps. The time-lapse photography of the growth and feeding habits of these plants rivals any science fiction film ever made. Yet nature provides these creatures and time lapse allows us to view them with an expanded point of view.

The British group Oxford Scientific Film Institute went a long way in the 1950s and 1960s toward refining the scientific use of time-lapse photography, inspiring many filmmakers and scientists like

Photo by A. Taradel

Figure 1.13

Dr. John Ott, circa 1950. (Courtesy of John Ott Pictures, Inc., © 1973.)

Attenborough and Ron Fricke. In the early 1980s, American filmmakers Godfrey Reggio and Ron Fricke created a feature film based around the revealing qualities of time lapse. It was called *Koyaanisqatsi*. Most of the film was shot in the "four corners" of the western United States and in New York City. The use of time lapse is so effective that clouds can be seen as rushing currents of water and people traversing streets in New York look like pulsing blood in the veins of an urban environment.

The perspective of this film is so unlike anything we are used to seeing that it is easy to understand the message these filmmakers are creating without a word of dialog or narration. Technically, this footage is superior, utilizing motion-control cameras, varied shutter speeds, natural and artificial light, and dynamic compositions. The sound work of Philip Glass helps place this film in a category of its own that is unique, beautiful, and powerful. Time lapse continues to be used in all sorts of commercial and educational venues. It's an effect that represents the complimentary side of "high-speed photography." Instead of slowing events down it speeds them up and presents a whole new way of observing any event.

There are numerous contemporary artists who are using time lapse as a basis for their own artistic expression. Successful extensions of this art form include Ken Murphy's multiple screen *History of the Sky* and the wonderful tilt/shift lens time lapse and "undercranked" work of Keith Loutit. Worlds are created where real-life scenes have the illusion of appearing like toys. Other examples are the collage

1. What Are the Possibilities?

time-lapse work of artists like Fong Qi Wei and Julian Tryba, knitting together various time exposures of scenes into one film.

The last alternative stop-motion technique that we will cover has many sub-categories of its own. The one element that unifies these various subcategories is the way they are shot. Materials like sand, beads, candy, paper, photographs, and an infinite list of objects all can be manipulated under a mounted camera on an animation stand or "down-shooter." This can also be referred to as a "multiplane" animation stand. All of these elements can be shot in a horizontal fashion, but with a downshooter they are treated like animation cels or drawings on a traditional animation stand. When shot this way, these objects can be free of the constraints of gravity. The most developed and popular technique in this area is "cutout" animation. This is when drawings, photographs, and other flat two-dimensional objects are jointed together with rivets, string, wax, or other hinging devices to simulate animated movement. Although this leans much more in the two-dimensional world like drawn animation, it is, technically speaking, a form of stop-motion or frame-by-frame manipulation. The German artist Lotte Reiniger created one of the earliest examples of this form of stop motion. *The Adventures of Prince Achmed* was a feature film produced in 1926 using flat opaque materials like lead and cardboard. These forms were shaped and constructed to move on a flat piece of glass with lighting that came from behind the cutouts. This created a silhouetted effect that was enhanced with some limited color and various background materials to give a painterly look.

Cutout animation was one of the most popular techniques of animation, after drawing, for the first part of the twentieth century. It was a way to display a fair amount of detail without having to draw that detail over and over again. The Japanese utilized this approach through artists like Noburo Ofuji and Kihachiro Kawamoto. Applying individual and cultural techniques and styles to cutout animation added to the depth of this approach. Kawamoto traveled to Czechoslovakia in the early 1960s to work with Jiri Trnka in Prague, but Trnka encouraged him to pursue his own cultural history and create stories and artistic applications that were relevant to Japanese culture. Cutout animation was a fairly popular technique that was practiced by animators who worked in different mediums, including model stop-motion animation and traditional cel or drawn animation. Auteurs in Argentina, England, Russia, Czechoslovakia, the United States, and other countries created animations using back- and front-lighted cutouts, cardboard, lead, translucent color papers, illustrations, and engravings, among other materials. The films that were produced in cutouts tended to be figurative in nature and often had cultural and ethnic themes. The relatively low cost of production using this technique allowed independent filmmakers and financially challenged countries to compete on the world stage in animation. The late twentieth century had several successful applications of cutout animation. Most notable was the Russian Yuri Norshtein and his film *Tale of Tales*, produced in 1979. This is a haunting tale of a family, community, and the effects of war. Norshtein uses drawings and cutouts, superimposed layer upon layer, to create a very dreamy and often frightening memory

Figure 1.14

Yuri Norshtein working on THE OVERCOAT © 2000. Photograph by Maxim Granik. (Courtesy of Yuri Norshtein and Maxim Granik.)

full of atmosphere. This is a very controlled and time-consuming technique and Norshtein is one of the masters. He continues to work today on a feature called *The Overcoat*, which has been over 30 years in the making (Figure 1.14).

Other contributions to cutout animation include Terry Gilliam's work in the British television series *Monty Python's Flying Circus*. Gilliam, an expatriate American artist, cobbled together strange, surreal, and entertaining animated shorts for the series featuring drawings of his own and a large collection of Victorian illustrations and photographs animated together using the cutout approach. They were so offbeat and unusual that his animation became a signature part of the series (Figure 1.15).

In more recent history, there have been several American television shows that started out as cutout animation but evolved into computer-generated images that simulate the cutout approach. *South Park*, created by Trey Parker and Matt Stone, was first conceived in cutout animation but became too difficult to produce in volume using this technique. There have been many more pieces of animation for television and the Internet that mimic the cutout look but use computer animation for efficiency, including *Blue's Clues*, JibJab animation, and *Angela Anaconda*. The 2008 Israeli animated feature film *Waltz with Bashir* is great example of how sophisticated modern cutout techniques have become with the use of computers and multilayering composite work.

These examples of cutout animation primarily use flat illustrated or photographic elements, but a downshooter can also manage to hold more dimensional objects like beads, candy, clay, sand, or any other object that can fit between the shooting surface and the mounted camera. Two examples of this approach are from the 1988 film *Candyjam*, directed by Americans Joan Gratz and Joanna Priestley. It features the work of animators from around the world and is themed

Figure 1.15

Two-legged Teddy Roosevelt, *Monty Python's Flying Circus*, Terry Gilliam, circa 1970. (Courtesy of Roger Saunders. © Python Pictures Ltd, 1969.)

around candy. Several of the animators animated candy on a glass surface in patterns and figurative forms. There's a wonderful mix between flat and dimensional styles that helps make this rich in texture and style.

Sand on glass is another popular downshooting technique that was mastered by the American-born Carolyn Leaf. Although Leaf was born and educated in the United States, she is associated with the National Film Board of Canada, where she produced numerous films throughout the 1970s and 1980s and into the twenty-first century. Sand is manipulated on a flat glass surface with the camera mounted directly above the glass. The lighting comes from below the glass and the sand blocks the light from the camera, leaving a silhouetted image. The thinner the layer of sand the more light comes through, giving the image a feathered look. There are many variations on this technique and Leaf employs them well (Figure 1.16).

We have only touched on a bit of the history and highlights of these alternative stop-motion photographic techniques. Filmmakers have always been fascinated by the potential of creating images frame by frame to create illusions and fantasy. Although the majority of animation artists have followed a more figurative and narrative approach to animation and stop motion in particular, there are many successful examples of less traditional, alternative uses of the medium in the non-figurative areas. Today artists are revisiting some of these older techniques and putting a new spin on them with fresh ideas and technology. A real image that is captured by a camera has a unique and genuine appeal that is hard to deny. Computer imagery is full, fluid, and quite refined but it is the imperfection and anomalies of the photographic expression of an object or person that strikes us

Figure 1.16

Carolyn Leaf working with sand on glass. (Courtesy of the National Film Board of Canada, Montreal, Quebec, Canada.)

to the core. The process of shooting photographic frame-by-frame films requires a certain skill set that is unique to these techniques. The innovators that we have mentioned in this chapter have all been groundbreakers. They have had to take risks to experiment and use what they have discovered in their process and expand upon those discoveries. Many, like Dziga Vertov, were not very readily accepted in society, but their passion and drive to discover new means of expression in their filmmaking drove them forward in their frame-by-frame approaches. Pixilation, time lapse, and downshooting are techniques that exemplify this approach, and we will explore them in more depth in the following chapters. The possibilities are expansive.

2

Shooting Frame by Frame

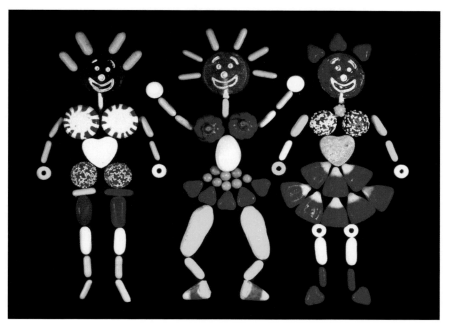

Candyjam © 1988 Joanna Priestley and Joan Gratz. (Courtesy of Joanna Priestley.)

Technique to Serve the Idea
Preproduction
Equipment and Setting Up

Technique to Serve the Idea

A lot of people are trigger-happy—they just want to be shooting/animating all the time because it makes them feel like they are being productive. But in reality, you are just wasting creative energy if you haven't done the hard work on your ideas. And it is hard work. There are days when you smash your head against a wall trying to work something out. I spend a lot more time refining my ideas than I actually spend shooting.

To me, understanding that your ideas are what make you unique is the most important thing. There are many people who can shoot or animate well. That's not the rare thing. A good idea is the rare thing.

PES

I am always torn between the excitement of jumping directly into the production of an animated idea and approaching an idea with a more well-thought-out plan. Getting your hands on a camera and simple capture software and shooting a scene spontaneously can be fresh and exhilarating until you run into your first challenge or "problem." This is especially true when shooting frame-by-frame pixilation of human subjects. Any animation is hard work and you don't want to waste anyone's time and energy. Creative ideas need to be drafted and carefully honed to impress any audience these days. We are a visual storytelling society and much more discerning about filmmaking language than at any other time. Having a good idea and an interesting way of telling it will gain and hold an audience's attention, and that's good communication. This planning phase, known as "pre-production," will be your road map or core idea that will give you direction. Your idea will also change and evolve, and that's not a bad thing. There is room for the spontaneous approach, mentioned earlier, in this process and we will come across that subject again later on.

The first step in any film is the idea. What do you want to say? What idea, story, or visual art do you want an audience to receive? Who is your audience? Do you even care that an audience will see your work? There are many filmmakers who have no care for what an audience thinks. These "artists" want to only explore their own vision as best they can to their own satisfaction. This approach requires more risk if you are approaching filmmaking as a means of income. However, some of the most successful ideas come from this original thought process. The great majority of filmmakers do care what an audience thinks and tailor their approach to filmmaking to make a connection with the audience. They yearn for a laugh, a gasp, or a tear in reaction to their film. Getting your ideas down on paper can be challenging. Scriptwriting is not an innate talent that most filmmakers possess. It takes practice, guidance, and crafting. There are many books on this subject, so we won't go into this area. Ideas are another matter. I find that the old saying that "life is stranger than fiction" rings true. When you draw from your own experiences and the experiences of others that you know, then you may have a kernel of idea that can germinate. The effective outcome of this approach is that if you have had an experience and have reacted to it in some emotional way, then audiences have a greater access to empathy and your idea because we all share the human experience. Empathy, not sympathy, is a key ingredient to including an audience. We need to understand a character's emotion based on our own experiences, but we don't necessarily have to agree with that emotion.

The next step is to take advantage of the process and strengths of animation. Hyperbole or exaggeration and strong images can be used effectively in animation. When real human subjects are not being used as the subject matter, then we can address sensitive issues (like sex, death, and the human condition) with human proxies like animals, aliens, or even everyday objects. You can elicit human emotions and experiences through inanimate objects and get an audience to understand your point. The audience can understand the empathized point and not necessarily feel directly or personally targeted by the subject matter. This is true even in pixilation, the animation of humans, since the movement is unreal or unnatural (Figures 2.1 through 2.3).

There are many ways to approach ideas, and the subject is a book unto itself. The important thing to remember is what you want to say, who your audience is, and how your idea can be clearly expressed through animation. The great Czech master Jan Svankmajer approaches ideas and process in a less formal way.

I try to work spontaneously, I let the creative process open to chance and automatism.

Jan Svankmajer

Once you have an idea, then you need to think about an animated technique that will serve the idea or enhance it. For example, if a lawyer was going to demonstrate to a courtroom the events of an alcohol-induced fatal car accident to

Figure 2.1

Image by Lindsay Berkebile from *Meat!*. (Courtesy of Lindsay Berkebile © 2010.)

Figure 2.2

Image by PES from *Human Skateboard* for Sneaux Shoes. (Courtesy of PES Productions LLC, Wilmington, DE, © 2007.)

Figure 2.3

Image by Tom Gasek from "4 at 60" (working title, 2017).

prove his client's innocence, he or she would be best off using an emotionless, naturalistic, demonstration with computer-generated images. Imagine what the results would be if the lawyer showed this demonstration in clay animation or even pixilation. The courtroom might burst into laughter and not take the demonstration seriously. That lawyer would lose the case.

What would Gumby or Wallace and Gromit look like in drawn animation? Many of the old cartoons from the 1950s and 1960s are being updated into computer effects and images, and it just doesn't sit right. Some of this incongruity has to do with the way a film or character was first conceived. Originally, the choice of some techniques may have had more to do with economics than a technique to support the idea. Once a technique is established and an audience embraces that film or character, then it is treading on thin ice to move a beloved idea or character to a new animation approach. Ultimately, it is important to think about films that have been done using certain techniques and to consider why those techniques were used. If you chose to use pixilation, time lapse, or downshooting techniques', then how will that approach affect your final idea and outcome? Terry Gilliam from *Monty Python's Flying Circus* makes the following claim:

> I think the limitations of cutouts leads towards comedy or violence. Movements are crude, ungainly, and inelegant. It's hard to be portentous or pretentious with this technique. However, serious ideas can often be communicated very powerfully with humor. (Figure 2.4.)

Terry Gilliam

Today cutout animation is simulated with After Effects, Toon Boom, TVPaint, or Flash to smooth out the "violent" approach that Gilliam cites. As a result, more and more kids' shows are being produced this way. The movement is much more fluid and subtle.

Figure 2.4

Image from *Monty Python's Flying Circus*, Terry Gilliam. (Courtesy of Roger Saunders © Python Pictures Ltd, 1969.)

Pixilation has a tendency to also be "crude, ungainly, and inelegant" by the nature of the process. It is practically impossible to keep a human subject completely still or registered in the same position from one frame to the next. The result is a highly active frame that has a bit of a humorous and kinetic appeal. A pixilated Shakespeare would not be a great match (unless humor or parody is what you are seeking).

Time-lapse photography, which requires a consistent exposure of frames over a period of time, has a completely different effect. Events are sped up dramatically so time feels compressed into a short time span. When a time-lapse camera is pointed at the sky during an oncoming thunderstorm, the results can truly be awesome. Clouds look like waves of ocean water and one can see the power of nature (Figure 2.5).

When the time-lapse camera is focused on human subjects or animals, then the effect can be a bit more humorous. The fast and unnatural movements remind us of early films when cameras were "under-cranked" and you would see comedic action like the incompetent Keystone Kops from Mack Sennett in the early 1900s. Cameras used to be hand cranked or driven, so the number of frames that were exposed per second in the camera was less than the number of frames that were projected per second on a screen later. More action was packed into less time, which gave the effect of everything being sped up (Figures 2.6 and 2.7).

There are many ways to overcome the inherent features of a particular technique, and these adaptations to the technique will be one of the areas we explore in the chapters about each technique. It is important to think about what a technique might bring to a film and whether it is complementary to the concept of

Figure 2.5

Mount Zion landscape and clouds. (Courtesy of Eric Hanson © 1995.)

2. Shooting Frame by Frame

Figure 2.6

An old hand-cranked camera. (Museum of the Moving Image, photograph by Tom Gasek.)

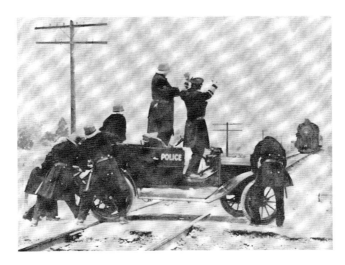

Figure 2.7

Keystone Kops, Mack Sennett's "Keystone Kops" circa 1915. (Courtesy of University of Oklahoma Press, Norman, OK, 1968.)

Figure 2.8

Image from the set of *Stanley Pickle*, with director Victoria Mather. (Courtesy of *Victoria Mather* © 2010.)

the film. If it is not complementary, then how can you adjust the technique to complement your idea? Once you have your idea and the proper technique, and in our case we are concentrating on these alternative stop-motion techniques, then you need to proceed deeper into preproduction.

> Making a film is huge opportunity and responsibility. Use the time and money wisely, and plan, plan, plan (Figure 2.8).

Vicky Mather (Director of Stanley Pickle)

Preproduction

Your concept and script need to be translated into visual language in order for you to know how to prepare for a shoot. This is the storyboard. Storyboarding can be a career unto itself, and there are some highly talented people who work in this arena. The critical job of the storyboard is to force you to think through your idea carefully, map out a plan of production, and help communicate it to people who will be involved in the production. The storyboard does not have to be beautiful. It needs to be practical and to communicate your idea visually. If you're creating a film for a potential client, especially one who may not have the visual imagination that you have, then making a well-rendered and clear storyboard becomes essential. If you are making a film for yourself or a few friends to help you in production, then a thumbnail or simple stick-figure rendering of your idea will suffice (Figure 2.9).

Figure 2.9

Thumbnail boards by Janine Carbone. (Courtesy of Janine Carbone © 2009.)

The use of reference material in this phase is a must. What does a Gila monster look like? What is the scale relationship between the Empire State Building and an igloo? What color is Mars? If you don't have any idea, then jump on the web and get some photographs and images to become informed. You can then distort this information, but you need to know the truth before you go off on a tangent. Even if you are creating something that has never been seen before, you may still need some reference for texture, details, or color. Reference material is where it all starts visually. If you don't draw very well and can't get someone to help you, then you might consider creating a photographic storyboard with a digital still camera. This approach requires that you go out and find images that you can photograph with your digital single lens reflex (DSLR) still camera or smartphone camera, or you can find images from magazines, the web, or other visual resources. By using some simple cutting and pasting in a program like Photoshop, you can create your own storyboard that clearly communicates the narrative or ideas that you need to show to tell your story. This is especially appropriate for the production of a pixilated film. Between reference material and photographs, you can create a storyboard that reminds you of how you planned the production and communicate this to your small crew (Figure 2.10).

Drawing is a great skill and one that I would encourage, but if the skill is not available then there are other ways to lay out a storyboard and move your production ahead. Storyboarding for time lapse and certain pixilated films may be close to impossible to draw out because it relies so much on the eye of the cinematographer and director when on location. Simply writing down shot ideas in sequence and what you want to accomplish with each shot can be very helpful. You then have to be open to what happens in the field. In time-lapse animation, it is absolutely critical to observe the event that you want to photograph. You need to know how long an event takes to unfold, what the subjects will do, how the lighting might change, and how the general environment, like the weather, might change before you shoot the final shot. You need to scout a location first. If you cannot scout a location or event before you shoot a time lapse, then you need to

Figure 2.10

A photographic storyboard.

get information about the weather, accessibility of the location, and what sort of traffic crosses through your focused area. This research and environmental anticipation can be done on the web or by talking to people who have been in the area that you want to shoot. This is all preproduction or the planning and preparation that is necessary to execute before you enter the actual production stage. It will save you a lot of time and effort and will help give clarity to your idea. It forces you to think through the process and problem-solve before the problems arise (which will happen in the field or on the downshooter during the actual shooting). Preproduction will not eliminate all of these potential problems but it will resolve the majority of them and it will focus your vision. Alternative stop-motion techniques are not an exception to all other types of animation when it comes to preproduction.

Many directors and animators like to take their preproduction process one step further. They make a moving storyboard, or what's known as an "animatic." This is when you put all of the storyboard panels into a timeline and make a movie of your artwork. It should be timed out to match the final timing of your film. You can make adjustments to the animatic and it will help determine the final cut of your animated film. Often animation can be pre-edited through this process. The advantage of this is that you don't overshoot the animation footage, which is a very time-consuming, expensive, and potentially exhausting experience. It will force you to look at the overall flow of your film and check for consistencies and will give you an idea of the dynamics of your shots all together. It's critical to look at the big picture. Once you capture the final footage, then the corresponding artwork shot for the animatic can be replaced by the final animated footage. The sound and dialog play an important role in this process (Figure 2.11).

One step that I practice and encourage all alternative stop-motion animators to consider is shooting some test footage before actual production begins. If you are pixilating someone, then try the action yourself in front of the camera and get a sense of the pace, action, and timing. Try your actor out in a test and give him or her a chance to practice this arduous technique, so you can see how they act and how you want the ultimate action to look. This is the time to have a bit

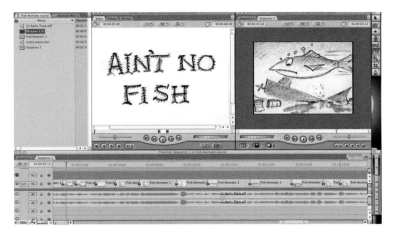

Figure 2.11

Animatic on a movie timeline (Final Cut, Adobe Premiere etc.).

more confidence with your shots, because you can't make any mistakes in a test. Allow yourself the spontaneity that can often birth new and exciting ideas that can be applied to your film. If you don't have someone to help you test a pixilated idea, then set your camera to run on a time-lapse interval and test a particular movement on your own. If you're looking to shoot a time-lapse event, then take your time-lapse camera and shoot a test of an event and see whether you need to consider an adjustment to your exposure or interval between exposures. Cutouts or sand on glass have their own properties, and a trial run will inform your initial animation shots and improve your technique right out of the gate. There is often a tendency to jump right into production shooting and no time is allowed for testing. I can't tell you how many times I have heard animators complain about their initial shots because they were learning everything on the first shots and then made adjustments in later shots. The desire to reshoot first shots is strong, but often schedules won't allow this. Testing can resolve this issue. There really is no reason not to test and experiment before you commit to your final film. Make sure to plan time for testing in your schedule before the production so it is not forgotten.

Testing requires equipment, and this is one more issue that needs to be addressed before final production begins. Pixilation and time-lapse animation utilize equipment that is familiar to live-action filmmakers. Cameras, computers, tripods, lights, and grip equipment like flags, C-stands, sandbags, and gaffer's tape can all be used with these alternative stop-motion techniques. The downshooter will require an animation stand, and this crosses over into the more traditional animation realm. All alternative stop-motion techniques have a camera as the primary piece of equipment. After all, we are stopping the camera frame by frame and manipulating the images in front of the camera, whether on a tripod or a downshooter, very much like the first "trick films."

In a recent interview with stop-motion artist PES, he discussed making his own work while producing commercials or working for compensation. He, and many artists, must make a living but not at the sacrifice of their own original work. This independent film work is often what feeds the artist creatively, which in turn can potentially lead to paid work. While planning your production, you should allow yourself the freedom to explore your own original ideas, vision, and approach. This can be defined by limited resources and budgets, but this challenges you to problem-solve, which is a key ingredient to stop-motion work. I often find that these original ideas are more potent than trying to create a contrived film idea for an intended audience. That is the job of commercial work. What appeals to your humor or what things do you want to visualize and explore? As mentioned earlier, this is a more "artistic" approach, which has risks if you are considering rewards or "success," but finding your own voice and style can be deeply satisfying. Stop-motion work, like any artistic venture including music, requires hours of practice and exposure. Like in a good workout, you break a sweat, and then you are on your way with confidence. A good idea will always win out over technique with any budget, and this is what you must strive for as you plan your preproduction.

Equipment and Setting Up

For decades, the movie film camera was the primary capture system. Kodak, Bell & Howell, and Mitchell cameras were steady and reliable animation cameras. Other cameras were used, but the key element that made a good stop-motion film camera was known as "pin registration." This basically meant that the camera had the ability to place the individual frame to be exposed in the exact same position in front of the film gate as the previous frame through placement pins. This eliminated the weave and bobbing up and down that could occur when films were projected (Figure 2.12).

These days, like many things, digital technology has put the animation film camera to rest. The two main digital cameras that are used are the digital video camera, including some webcams, and the DSLR camera. There are advantages to each camera and these will be explored in subsequent chapters. Remember that we need to have the ability to shoot one frame at a time. Digital still cameras are ideal for this approach because they were designed to take single still pictures. Most digital video cameras can be controlled to shoot single frames through the animation software that you will need to use. You can use a DSLR camera with a flash card and no capture software, but you will lose the ability to control the images from one to the next. All images that come through a digital camera are digitally registered in size and placement, so there will be a steady image when single frames are strung together to make a movie. Having a camera that has "manual" controls is critical for a steady image. Canon and Nikon are two leading brands in the DSLR arena, and Sony and Panasonic are two popular brands in the digital video approach. There are many more brands that work well and satisfy the requirements of alternative stop-motion techniques (Figure 2.13).

Figure 2.12

Mitchell camera with pins.

Figure 2.13

A digital video camera and a digital still camera.

As technology has evolved, the smartphone has become another option for all levels of filmmakers. The latest versions, the iPhone 7, iPhone 7 Plus, Samsung GS7, and the LG V20, are all examples of smartphones that have excellent cameras and lenses that, along with application software, can make excellent animated films. The decision you have to make as a cameraperson is whether you want to have your phone mounted on a tripod or handheld. Most studio and most "field" stop-motion shoots require a stable camera and the smartphone is no different. There are mini tripods and large tripod mounts for smartphones, so you can use your regular tripod with the mount adapter. If you choose not to use a tripod, then you have a very active image from frame to frame. This can work quite well if you keep some sort of loose registration from one image to the next by using your best judgment. I like to shoot handheld stop motion with objects or environments that have distinctive features so it's easier to gauge the placement of those objects in the frame from image to image. Using a smartphone as a sketchbook for ideas and movement tests can be quick and effective. Often I may see something, hand-hold a frame-to-frame shooting sequence, and then decide if I want to shoot that scene again in a more controlled manner. Web applications include stop-motion software that allows frame-by-frame capturing. Keep in mind that the videos that come from these smartphone devices may be compressed and will not look good if projected onto a large screen. You can often shoot time-lapse with the photo or camera function of one of these smartphones, but there is usually no control on the lapsed time between exposures. You will get a higher resolution video this way but at a loss of control of the shutter timer. One fun exercise to try with no capture software is what I call the "selfie cycle." Hold your camera away from your head and shoulders as if you were taking a selfie. Keep the camera and your head in the same relationship and position but turn your body about 20 degrees and take a frame for each 20-degree turn until you come back to the beginning position. Make sure your head looks like it's in the same position in each frame. Download these frames into a program like Premiere or After Effects and play it back on loop for the cycle effect. You can also use an application like Stop Motion Studio for this exercise (Figure 2.14).

The computer software that makes animation possible and easier to execute is known as "capture software." There are several different brands, and they are listed on our associated website and mentioned through-out this book. Dragonframe and Stop Motion Pro are ubiquitous across the globe. New brands like Pinnacle Studio are entering the marketplace. I use Stop Motion Studio as

Figure 2.14

Images from a selfie cycle by Tom Gasek, 2016.

2. Shooting Frame by Frame

an app on my smartphone. There are several features that are common to all good capture software. They need to show you a "live" frame coming directly in from your camera. The ability to compare the previously captured frame and the live frame allows you to monitor the amount of movement your subject has registered. It's important to be able to step through all of your frames one frame at a time, so you can see the sequence of movement. The software needs to have instant playback at various frame rates so you can see your final animation. The better capture software programs have many more features that allow you to refine your animation and animation technique. They will also work on Apple and PC platforms. There are several inexpensive and free capture software programs like iStopMotion, FrameThief, MonkeyJam, Stop Motion Animator, and Anasazi that are available for novice animators. However, these programs can have support, technical, and capability limitations and may frustrate the more advanced stop-motion animator. They are great starter programs but are not quite up to the depth of the previously mentioned programs (Figure 2.15).

Similar to live-action photography and live-action moviemaking, all stop motion requires a "grip" package. This may include tripods, lights, flags, electric cords, voltage regulators for lights, sandbags, gaffer's tape, and potentially motion control for moving the camera (Figure 2.16). We will explore these elements in more detail, but it is important to know what is required by your particular script or idea. Naturally, for downshooting, an animation stand is required, but the stand may come in various forms. This can range from a classic Oxberry animation stand right down to a camera on a tripod pointed down at 45 degrees toward a tabletop. The Oxberry animation stand is like the Rolls Royce of downshooters. It offers weight, stability, and very accurate and dependable registration systems like machined peg bars used to perfectly match one cel or drawing to the next.

Figure 2.15

Screenshot of Dragonframe interface.

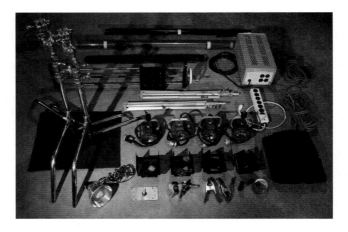

Figure 2.16

Grip equipment (lights, flags, voltage regulator, C-stands).

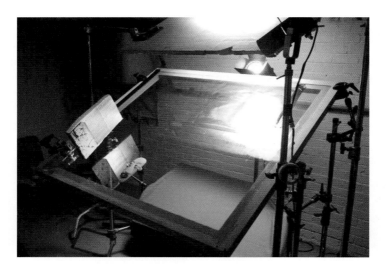

Figure 2.17

WONKY Films downshooter. (Courtesy of Wonky Films, Bristol, UK, © 2015.)

Often Oxberry stands, which are designed for both 16 mm and 35 mm film cameras, are computer controlled with stepping motors that drive the various components of the stand, like the shooting table, the lighting, and the mounted camera. Most downshooting producers custom build their own stand for a fraction of the cost of an Oxberry and it suits their needs quite well (Figure 2.17).

During this preplanning/preproduction process, you will need to think through all of your shots and determine the most efficient and effective way to shoot your production. You will examine your budget, space to shoot (if it requires a controlled studio environment), and the amount of time that you have to shoot.

Let's now move into one of the most popular forms of alternative stop motion. Pixilation can be direct and simple when practiced by novice filmmakers or it can be very sophisticated. Of all the various types of stop motion, pixilation can be a bit more spontaneous in production because it is very hard to control humans frame by frame. If you're out in the field it's hard to control any natural light and any peripheral activity. With the proper planning, observation, and application of this technique, the results can be very satisfying and fresh.

3

Pixilation

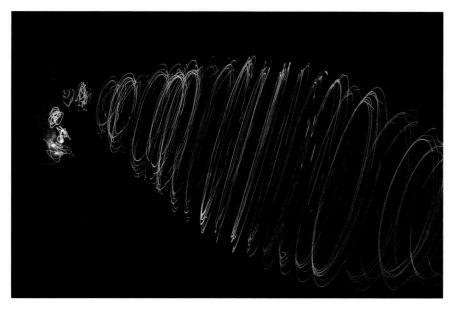

Light painting created with colored Christmas lights by Tom Gasek.

Take Advantage of the Medium

We like the fact that you can feel the real material in the objects. When you choose your medium of work you get another aspect to play with. How that material would express what I want to express? When you animate a paper or a person you actually use a material that everybody has a relation to, and then you add another layer and give this material life in any way your imagination will lead you.

Merav and Yuval Nathan

Pixilation is one of the most popular techniques for anyone who wants to jump right into animation with little or no experience. Having a camera is about all that is necessary to begin this process. Naturally, there are more possibilities if you have a well-thought-out idea, a computer, capture software, and a tripod, but capturing images on a compact disk in the camera and the ability to sequence those pictures into a movie is all it really takes to shoot a pixilated film. Even an experienced stop-motion animator can pare down his or her equipment to a single camera or smartphone and create an interesting film. Having some knowledge of how to take advantage of this technique will make a huge difference in the final outcome. The early "trick film" artists like Melies knew how to utilize the unique qualities of single-frame manipulation and add a sense of drama. We will explore some of these tricks and advantages of pixilation in this chapter, not just the equipment but the ideas and execution of your next pixilated film.

What exactly is "pixilation?" Remember that it was Grant Monroe, who worked with Norman McLaren on *Neighbours*, who coined this term. Monroe and McLaren used the human body as the animated subject. Unlike model animation, pixilation—or the animation of humans—requires no intensive model building, armature building, or even character designing. Everyday objects like kitchen appliances, cars, books, or any premade physical form can be moved or animated frame by frame and this would also be considered pixilation, which is a subdivision of stop motion. Animating humans with their inherent armature or skeleton appears to be the most frequently used subject of pixilated films. As you can imagine, the variations are limitless.

If you start to add the elements of design or makeup to people in a pixilated film, then the results can be even more dramatic. This is what McLaren did in *Neighbours* and what Jan Kounen emulated in his 1989 film *Gisele Kerozene* (Figure 3.1).

The addition of makeup or costuming enhances the dramatic effect of the film but so can the strong expressions of the pixilated human figures. This is not a delicate and subtle animation technique because human subjects are always moving. It is virtually impossible for humans to stand absolutely still like a model or an object so the result is an impulsive energy and vibration. To overcome this effect of internal energy, the expressions of a human subject need to be bold and powerful. The eye is drawn to the strong expression and becomes less concerned about the constant vibration of movement, which can be a potential distraction. Once you understand this principle, then you can experiment with variations of

Figure 3.1

Still image from *Neighbours* (Grant Munro). (Courtesy of National Film Board of Canada, Montreal, Quebec, Canada, © 1952.)

expression and constant movement. Lindsay Berkebile, a young filmmaker in the Los Angeles area, puts it this way:

> In my film, *MEAT!* I took a simple concept and used the stylized movement pixilation provides to my advantage. The movement is exaggerated; the facial expressions are pushed to the limit and place an audience at an uneasy state. The movement, especially in this piece, is very controlled for pixilation. There are a lot of pauses, silent moments, and breaths throughout the film. However, the stillness still has a vibrating life to it, which I feel gives the film a sort of chaotic life amongst silence.
>
> **Lindsay Berkebile**

In my own 2009 film, *Off-Line*, I wanted to animate a real human arm and hand pressing a microwave's start button. I wanted a slightly affected movement, but I desired a more fluid live-action approach to the movement of the hand. I ended up making a support or rig to hold the human subject's arm so I could control the movement. If the support was not there, then the inward movement of the arm would have been less direct and effective (Figure 3.2).

So setting up rigs, using predetermined staging marks, and designing the look of a character through makeup and strong expressions can add a whole other layer to your pixilated film.

Knowing how to use pixilation, especially with human subjects, can really complement the emotional or visual storytelling aspect of your filmmaking. Ultimately, there are several things that are unique to pixilation. Since each frame is taken one at a time with an indeterminate period of time between frames,

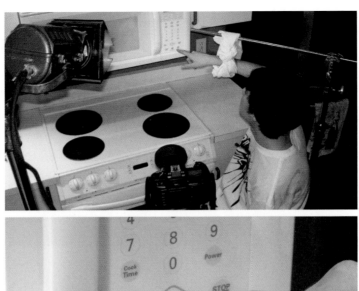

Figure 3.2

Tyler Gasek with arm-support rig, *Off-Line*, 2009 by Tom Gasek.

there is the ability to completely rearrange or manipulate your subject matter and frame. This could come in the form of removing or introducing an object or person from one frame to the next, capturing the movement or position of an individual as with a midair jump for each frame, or just bringing inanimate objects to life. These are the same principles that the early trick film artists utilized and that are just as effective today. These techniques have a unique quality when done photographically, eliciting a sense of magic.

Who Is the Director?

When animating a pixilated film, there are at least two important roles that need to be addressed. One is the person behind the camera, or the director, and the other is the person(s) in front of the camera, or the actor. At least one of these people must have a basic understanding of animation. The principles of easing in and out of movement, of accelerated action, secondary motion, anticipation, overlapping action, squash and stretch, and the effects of momentum add a lot of dynamism and interest to any scene. To review these principles, let's look at a few illustrations. When any movement begins, it takes a lot of energy to make an object break inertia. There is an acceleration of movement frame to frame as the object (person) gains speed. The opposite is true when an object comes to a stop. The object decelerates. Think of when you drive a car and how it works. You step on the accelerator, forcing the tires to start rotating and getting up to cruise speed, where the tires rotate at an even rate, giving the car an even speed; then you apply the brakes to slow down the rotation of the tires and the distance you travel before you come to a complete stop. When the tires stop turning, the car continues slightly forward with secondary motion and then the chassis settles back to its default position directly over the tires. Once this principle is understood, the director or actor can break these rules and create some different effects (Figure 3.3).

"Secondary motion" basically means that any appendage or secondary mass like hair on a head or the tail of an animal will trail behind the main body of movement. For example, if a person quickly turns his or her head, the hair will trail a few frames behind the mass of the head, which is the source of the movement. The head will stop, but the hair will continue around past the head's stationary position and then settle down (Figure 3.4).

Figure 3.3

The basic physics of any movement require ease-in and ease-out movements with an accelerated increase and decrease in the amount of movement for each frame.

Figure 3.4

Secondary motion of hair as it trails behind the turn of a head.

Figure 3.5

The wind-up or anticipation allows an audience time to focus on an object before it moves, and anticipation builds energy just before that action occurs.

"Anticipation" basically means in order to move in a particular direction you must first move slightly in the opposite direction. This wind-up builds energy and allows the audience to see what is about to happen for a beat before it actually happens. This is exaggerated in animation but often does happen in real life (Figure 3.5).

"Squash and stretch" is an exaggeration of the way movement occurs and how weight and form shifts within that movement. Again it is emphasized in animation and can add a humorous element when it is highlighted. These classic principles of animation apply to pixilation as much as any other form or technique of animation. It is limited with the human body because the body can only be stretched and squashed within its physical limits, but this principle can still be applied (Figure 3.6).

Figure 3.6

The human figure can squash and stretch for a humorous effect, but it is limited in its physical range.

All of these basic principles should be considered when producing pixilation. Applying these guides to movement must be planned and intentionally done. After all, how can you have a head of hair fly around a turning head when you are shooting one frame at a time and there is no momentum to make the hair fly? Gravity will pull the hair down. In this case, if you want to have the hair flying, you may have to consider using hair spray in each frame, after arranging the hair in a particular position of movement, or use some sort of rig that is weaved through the hair or clear fishing line to hold the hair while the slow process of shooting single frames occurs. We will discuss rigs and special requirements further in this book. Many pixilation artists use live-action footage for this kind of effect and then mix and match it in with the pixilated footage, because rigs can be very challenging to control.

You may decide that you don't want that kind of natural movement and let pixilation be pixilation with all of its particular attributes. The bottom line is that these are decisions that must be made and the director is the one who will plan the shoot and make the calls. It is possible to simultaneously be a director and an actor who performs in front of the camera, but there are limitations to this approach. You can't really see what the camera is seeing and although you might be able to judge the kind of movement that is required for each frame of an action, you will not be able to adjust your position or registration in the frame relative to the previously captured frame. Naturally, you can set up a computer or have your computer attached to a projector in front of you so you can see yourself as you animate yourself. The problem is that you will be concentrating on looking at yourself and not necessarily on what you need to concentrate on. There are also wireless remote controls with infrared beams that allow you to shoot your camera from across the room, but this takes careful control and aim and might pull you out of position. Finally, you can use a time-lapse feature on your camera, but that requires that you be ready for your next position every frame within that allotted time interval. So you can be an actor and a director simultaneously, but it is much more effective to have someone behind the camera shooting and calling out to you or actually moving you as the animated (actor) subject.

Humor

Although pixilation has been explored since Norman Mclaren work in the 50's, it had tended to be used largely for slapstick effect. Our initial interests were in trying to use the technique in a more-subtle and expressively dramatic way.

The intention was to make a film that looked like live action but (moved) like an animation film. When successful, the technique creates a distorted realism that can very effectively be used to accentuate or exaggerate a character's personality and presence. It was that possibility of manipulating the dramatic performance of a character that led to the use of pixilation techniques in the Tom Thumb project.

Dave Borthwick (Bolex Brothers), *The Secret Adventures of Tom Thumb*

As Dave Borthwick points out, many pixilated films have leaned into humor and slapstick primarily because the fast and energetic movement of pixilation tends to strike the funny bone. Yet this technique of animating people also lends itself to more serious subject matter. The more expression and movement are controlled, the more serious the effect can be. As Lindsay Berkebile points out, using holds with as little movement as possible in a human animated subject can emote a sense of quiet desperation or an inner energy and conflict that may reveal another layer of interpretation in an animated performance. The key is in the performance, expression, and overall movement.

In Jan Kounen's *Gisele Kerozene* and in Norman McLaren's *Neighbours*, the action is so broad and absurd that one can't help but laugh. In *Neighbours*, when one of the battling men, played by Grant Monroe, hits the other neighbour's wife with a picket fence post, throws her baby to the ground and kicks the baby off-screen, we can't help but laugh despite the dark humor involved. It is so tragic that it actually becomes comedic and the fast pace action of the pixilation feeds the humor. As Terry Gilliam states:

… serious ideas can often be communicated very powerfully with humour.

Terry Gilliam

There are a few techniques that can be used to help smooth out the action of a performance, allowing for more serious interpretations. It appears that the more time is spent between frames adjusting people, the greater the potential for more quirky and misregistered movement to occur. This can be very funny looking. But if the movement of a character is smoother, then the effect can lean more towards serious interpretation. Expression and performance play a key role but we are concentrating strictly on movement. So if an actor being shot frame by frame moves slowly and constantly and the camera operator continuously shoots frames, capturing more evenly paced in-betweens of action, the action will be smoother, mimicking live-action movement. There should be a minimum of time spent between shot frames. The person being shot is moving constantly and will be better registered in placement from frame to frame as opposed to spending minutes between frames adjusting position and losing that registration.

Surprise is always an effective way to conjure up a good laugh. Pixilation allows a filmmaker the ability to change the subject matter or position of the subject within the frame for each shot. This erratic movement combined with unexpected action and subject placement within a frame is fun and surprising. That elicits humor. Quick movement that is similar to the animation in the work of Warner Bros. director Chuck Jones can raise a laugh. Treating human subjects like cartoons that whip across a frame and do the impossible (like dancing across a dance floor on their fingers, slamming into walls with no consequences, and other humanly impossible feats) make us laugh and think of these human subjects as unreal. This quick stylized movement is what Dave Borthwick was referring to when he mentioned that a lot of pixilation was relegated to the slapstick world.

One exercise that many animators must face is what is known as "lip sync." In animation, most often, final voice recordings are created before the animation occurs. The movement or animation is driven by the delivery of the voice. In puppet animation, the lips of the puppet are drawn, sculpted, manipulated by controllers or changed from one shape to another. All of the vowels and consonants in any dialog have their own assigned shape and those shapes must be integrated into the figure at the exact right frame count. The result is that the character model looks like they are actually saying the words (which have been previously recorded). Animators spend a lot of time doing this because the first step is to break down the dialog into frames. This is a slow laborious job that requires concentration and accuracy and very careful listening. Dragonframe has a feature, like many other software programs, that allows you to import final dialog into the timeline and see it in relationship to the picture frame count. There is also a waveform that is associated with that dialog. The animator or person breaking down the sound must listen (usually with headphones) to the dialog while watching the waveform. The dialog must be slowly "scrubbed" frame by frame so that each individual sound (vowel, consonant, or blend of the two) can be associated with a written letter or sound, which is then written down on a "log sheet," also known as a "dope sheet" or "exposure sheet." Suddenly you realize that animation, especially when lip sync is associated, is a very controlled and often predetermined art form. I am often amazed at the sound breakdown people that I have worked with on feature or TV series work. They work all day breaking down thousands and thousands of frames of sound day after day and yet, somehow, they remain sane! (Figure 3.7).

Pixilation can also utilize this approach to animated dialog. It takes a bit more concentration when it comes to the performance of the actor in front of the camera. We have already stated that exaggeration is an essential part of pixilation and that can also be applied to pixilated lip sync. Medium-wide and wide shots are not very effective for pixilated lip sync because the jittery activity of the body becomes too distracting for the viewer to see the lips moving properly. When the camera moves in for a close-up then we can start to play with this technique. The great thing about having the waveform associated with the dialog and written

Frame #	Dialogue	Sound (Music and SFX)	Actions 1	Actions 2	Camera Directions
1					
2					
3					
4					
5					
6					
7					
8			Open mouth		
9					
10	H	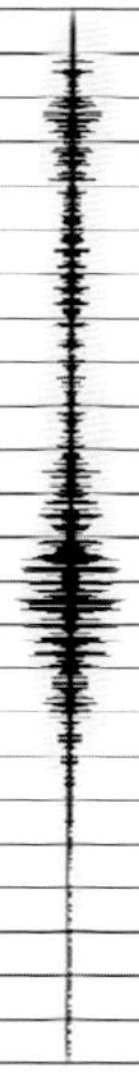			
11	~				
12	e				
13	~				
14	l				
15	l				
16	~				
17	~				
18	~				
19	~				
20	O				
21	~				
22	~				
23	~		Peak of "o"		
24	~				
25	~				
26	~		Taper out		
27	~				
28	~				
29					
30					
31					
32					
33					
34					
35					
36					

Figure 3.7

A log sheet with the word "Hello" broken down frame by frame.

breakdown of each word is that you can see where the energy lies in the delivery of the dialog. Greater dynamic range of the waveform means a more dynamic delivery of the dialog. Bigger body movements should be associated with bigger waveforms, because when you speak loudly it generally takes more diaphragm movement and body energy. Your human subjects should reflect that energy. The next area to focus on is the actual shape of the lips. The biggest mistake I see in puppet and non-puppet lip sync is over-animation or overactive movement in the lips and mouth shape. Simplify the shape of the lips, making sure to capture consonants with frame accuracy and always shoot two frames per lip shape, especially if you are shooting at 30 frames per second (FPS). I have animated puppets and people with as few as 8–10 mouth shapes for all dialog. This includes the dialog only, without expression. Remember that some shapes look very similar,

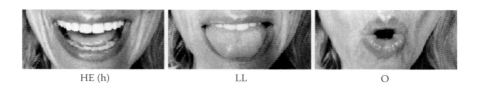

HE (h)   LL   O

Figure 3.8

A series of three lip-sync shapes from one second of dialog.

like *s* and *e* or *a* and *eh*. Breaking down the sounds phonetically, or as you actually hear them, and then writing that down on the log sheet in the proper frame line is critical. Finally, seriously consider exaggerating the lip shapes on your human subject, which often include the tongue and teeth, to help define certain consonants. This can be very humorous in the final result (Figure 3.8).

Shooting on Twos, Fours, and More

Often pixilation filmmakers will mix smooth and quirky misregistered movement together. This adds an interesting dynamic to the movement in a film. We just explored constant shooting of the single-frame camera but the mixture of live-action photography and pixilation can be very effective to achieve this dynamic. A great example of the mixture of frame rates is Norman McLaren and Claude Jutra's 1957 animated short called *A Chairy Tale*. McLaren and Jutra would often shoot at half-normal live-action speed (12 FPS) to speed up the action and blend that footage with the more time-consuming frame-to-frame manipulations (Figure 3.9).

Figure 3.9

Still from *A Chairy Tale*, Norman McLaren and Claude Jutra. (Courtesy of National Film Board of Canada, Montreal, Quebec, Canada, © 1957.)

Figure 3.10

The clay head of Mephisto from *Faust*, Jan Svankmajer. (Courtesy of Jan Svankmajer. Photo © Athanor Ltd Film Production Company, Jaromir Kallista and Jan Svankmajer.)

Another successful practitioner of the pixilation and live-action mix is Jan Svankmajer. It is blended so well that the viewer easily falls into the magical space that is created with these practical and photographic effects. In the 1994 film *Faust*, Svankmajer cuts back and forth between live action, pixilation, and clay models of Mephisto (Figure 3.10).

Jan Kounen did the same thing in *Gisele Kerozene* and claims:

> I'm no more thinking of stop motion as a genre, but only as a technique …, even in Gisele Kerozene, there is 20% of real stop motion the rest is shooting continuously at 2 frames a second, or 6 frames.

Jan Kounen

Both McLaren and Kounen were shooting with movie film cameras that allowed them to vary the shooting frame rate. The present-day digital still cameras now have the capability to shoot live-action movies and most newer models shoot in high definition. They are starting to include features such as variable frame rates like the Nikon D-7100, which shoots 6 FPS, and the Canon 7D Mark 2 or Mark 3, which can shoot 24, 30, and 60 FPS. Many digital video cameras have this various frame rate feature available because they were made to shoot live-action video. The digital still cameras are not far behind. Please refer to the associated website to see the latest in camera technologies.

For animators who don't have access to this higher-end equipment, using the continuous shooting technique will help vary the look of a pixilated film. When you shoot "pure" stop motion, or heavily manipulate the subject matter between frames, then you need to consider how many pictures or frames you want to use for every increment of subject movement. Since moving human subjects is physically challenging, it is best to reduce the amount of work demanded of them. I often shoot my human subjects at a rate of 15 FPS and play back the footage at 15 FPS. Or you can just shoot two pictures for every movement of the human subject and play it back at 30 FPS. This is known as "shooting on twos" and has the same effect as shooting at 15 FPS with a playback of 15 FPS. Because National Television System Committee video is 30 FPS, that is the rate I like to use. This is most common in the Americas and parts of East Asia. In film, the projected playback rate is 24 FPS and so many animators will shoot two pictures per movement played back at 24 FPS. But if this film is transferred to video, then there is an interpolation made to stretch those 24 frames into 30 FPS by averaging out two frames every five frames of footage. This works well but can be somewhat problematic if you are creating special effects frame by frame in postproduction where every frame needs to be a clean, distinctive image. In this case, images are worked on in the effects area at 24 FPS and then stretched to 30 FPS after the effects work is done.

Variations on Pixilation

Although the animation or pixilation of people is quite popular, so is the combination of people and 2D graphic elements, the animation of light, and the animation of everyday objects. Mixing people frame by frame with drawn animation, graphics, objects, and an infinite variation on this theme exemplify this last category of pixilation. The important element that distinguishes this approach is that these elements are combined directly in front of the camera and not in a postproduction process. One example of this approach is by the late filmmaker Jordan Greenhalgh, an independent filmmaker in New York. Jordan made a film called *Process Enacted* in which he shot his human subject frame by frame with a Polaroid camera and then animated the Polaroid photographic prints on a tabletop (Figures 3.11 and 3.12).

This is a time-consuming and difficult process because it requires twice the amount of animation, once for the human figure and once for the animation of the Polaroid photographs, but the results are fascinating. In this kind of approach, spontaneity of production can be risky so planning ahead reduces that risk. Jordan states:

> I test shoot every idea. I have to work out the technical kinks. I also storyboard and make animatics to get a feeling for the film as a whole ….

Jordan Greenhalgh

The contemporary, Italian-born graffiti artist and animator Blu has made several films featuring paintings on buildings that animate across an entire neighbourhood or urban environment. His animation is often shot in outdoor

Figure 3.11

Multiple Polaroid images for *Process Enacted*. (Courtesy of Jordan Greenhalgh © 2007.)

Figure 3.12

Second shot from *Process Enacted* (upright Polaroid). (Courtesy of Jordan Greenhalgh © 2007.)

environments where the natural movement of light helps keep his frame active and fluctuating in exposure. He then adds constant movement to his camera in an erratic fashion that infuses an energy and freshness to the image. There is an aesthetic choice to this approach as well as a practical advantage. Because the camera is moving constantly, the viewer accepts the active camera and consistent jittery motion, which helps mask any exposure, lighting, or camera placement changes. These changes may naturally occur due to weather, time, or unforeseen obstacles. This technique, like most stop motion, is difficult and time-consuming, and it may take days or weeks to complete single shots. He can stop in the middle of a shot at the end of one day and start back up several days later and the shift in the image will not stand out. It's impossible to control external conditions for any extended period of time outdoors and so Blu's aesthetic and practical solution works very well. Since the overall frame is so active, Blu creates strong, striking graphic images like in his 2008 film *Muto* and his 2010 film *Big Bang Big Boom*. The eye is drawn to the constantly morphing and moving image and is not distracted by the highly active overall frame. This contrast and focus of the eye is highly effective. In both films Blu moves his images from graphic, flat, painted images to three-dimensional forms that may carry some of the painted graphic elements on them as they move through the frame. Occasionally Blu will appear in and out of the frame, revealing some of the process of making the actual film (Figures 3.13 and 3.14).

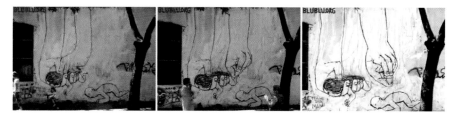

Figure 3.13

A series of three shots from *Muto* showing the movement in framing from one shot to the next. Directed by Blu. (Courtesy of Blu © 2008.)

Figure 3.14

Shots from *Big Bang Big Boom*, demonstrating the use of 2D and 3D elements shot frame by frame. Directed by Blu. (Courtesy of Blu © 2010.)

Light is an element that many contemporary artists are starting to rediscover. Light generally plays a big role in photographic frame-by-frame animation because it gives form to objects and sets atmosphere. Pixilation filmmakers create films both indoors and outdoors with controlled lighting and "wild" lighting, or lighting that occurs naturally. The sun is the largest light that we utilize, but human-generated lights, both in the studio and out in the streets, have great potential to be exploited. British pixilation artist Vicky Mather created a wonderful film called *Stanley Pickle*, which has a very inventive way of representing characters through action, camera movement, and lighting. The controlled interior world of Stanley Pickle's home is contrived and mechanical. The lighting is controlled and the movement of Stanley and his family are stiff and robotic. The camera is mostly static. Yet there is a world and a wood nymph outside the house, which have captured Stanley's attention and affection. The young woman moves freely in a sliding dance manner and the lighting is natural and wild in contrast to the interior world. The camera is free and moves through the scenes. In the end, Stanley makes a transition from his interior mechanical world to the freedom of the outside natural world. Mather uses pixilation to emphasize these contrasting worlds and how they collide, and the lighting, camera, and movement of the actors highlight these differences. Mather states (Figure 3.15):

> I like that it has a nostalgic quality to it that feels like a dream or a memory. I also appreciate being able to up and leave the studio—sit in a field and try something new. By embracing the elements; the cloud movement, the wind, the trees almost breathing. Uncontrollable natural elements make the stakes higher and you are forced to work within the unpredictability of the outdoors, so I'm faced with the challenge to find some sort of nuance that might look good in pixilation—I find it thrilling to take that risk and go with my gut instinct.
>
> **Vicky Mather**

Figure 3.15

Interior and exterior lighting scenes from *Stanley Pickle,* directed by Victoria Mather. (Courtesy of Victoria Mather © 2010.)

3. Pixilation

Figure 3.16

Tools required to light paint: camera, tripod, lights (LED, etc.), and colored gels.

Painting with light, frame by frame, has begun to expand with today's technology. By using LED lights or even bright flashlights in a dark environment you can create a light painting. Like the other techniques that we discussed, you must use a DSLR camera that has all manual controls on a tripod. By setting the shutter speed to a long exposure (at least 2 seconds and potentially longer), you can draw streaking light images frame to frame (Figure 3.16).

The light(s) must face the camera lens as you draw an outline or image. Since the room or exterior environment is dark, the light painter should wear dark clothes and may disappear from the final image all together. Most light painters are not afraid to leave a trace of their own image on the screen and there is a certain quality unique to light painting with this approach. You actually see the hand (and body) of the artist. Many times hiding the light painter is almost impossible because of the ambient and reflected light and long exposures. The images that are the most vivid are the light drawings and stable immobile objects in the frame, but if the light painter moves around while painting then his or her image blurs and becomes more ghostlike. A light that is bright and moving will leave a strong streak of color (if you use colored lights) that creates a drawn image on the frame. Some artists create images freehand for every frame. It's important to know the shape you are drawing and to be able to repeat it or potentially change that image frame to frame like any animation. You can have a person or cutout of the shape you want to draw as a guide when you light paint if you need that kind of consistency (Figure 3.17).

The opening image of this chapter is from an experiment I tried one holiday evening. I took a string of Christmas tree LED lights, plugged them into the wall, and had a person hold the plug tightly in the wall socket. I then took the other end, stretched it out, and started to swing the lights. I created an animated cycle where I pulled the lights out as far as I could and swung the lights during

Figure 3.17

Guide for light painting.

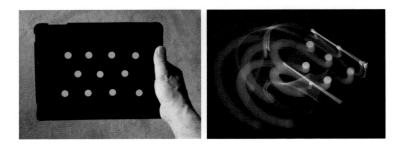

Figure 3.18

iPad being held in the dark to form a distinctive shape.

a 2- to 3-second exposure and then the next frame I loosened up the string by moving slightly closer to the socket with the lights. I swung them again creating a wider loop. So I went slightly wider with the light swing, took a frame, and then pulled the lights tighter away from the socket for a tighter loop so in the end I had a cycle of 12 frames of the lights swinging in a wide to tight loop and back to create the cycle.

New approaches to light painting include using iPads as the source of light. By predetermining certain shapes and colors, the light painters can move in the dark with their iPads in hand. The iPad image changes frame to frame and with the movement of the painter holding the iPad, and the combination of a long exposure allows words and more distinctive shapes to be extruded exposure by exposure. Motion control is another high-tech method for light painting. Lights are mounted on a computer-controlled platform and the movement is predetermined and executed by the motion control unit frame by frame, giving a very distinctive light impression (Figure 3.18).

The final area of pixilation that I want to cover is what I call "object animation." This is very close to model animation and is treated in a similar fashion. The main difference is that the objects have little or no manipulation performed on them. In puppet or model animation, there is sculpting, armature fabricating, molding, painting, and a whole series of processes that are involved before that model is put in front of the camera to allow it to operate in a very particular way

Figure 3.19

Several different sizes of candy corn used as replacement models imitating a flame. (Courtesy of PES © 2007.)

(like a figurative puppet). In object animation, there usually is very little done to the object. The animation of an object, how it is moved, is the way that expression and storytelling are achieved with this technique.

One of the most successful contemporary artists in this area is an American animator who calls himself "PES." Although not trained in animation, PES worked in the advertising industry around short-subject filmmaking (commercials). Some might consider PES a three-dimensional collage artist. In his first successful film, mentioned earlier in this book, PES animated real chairs on the roof of a New York City apartment building. This film, *Roof Sex*, has a strong sense of art direction in color and composition. The chairs, which have no human features, are moved in a way that mimics humans having coitus. Understanding the effects of movement through testing and reference film allows an animator to reproduce a particular action that may not normally be associated with that object. As humans we recognize certain actions associated with our species because we understand ourselves (mostly). Once that motion is translated into another object, we can identify with it and find interest and/or humor. PES has a simple trick that he uses on his website and in his 2009 film, *Western Spaghetti*. He mimics a flame, on a stove or in a fireplace on top of pretzels (which look like logs), by using several different sizes of pieces of candy corn and replacing them in front of the camera every two frames. It is so simple but so effective. This technique, which is known as "replacement" animation, calls for the substitution of one object for another similar but different object. The changing objects create an animated effect. This is one way to achieve squash and stretch in object animation. Replacement animation is one of the cornerstones of all stop-motion techniques. People can be substituted for people, objects can be substituted for other similar objects, and the effect can be magical as in the PES candy corn flames (Figures 3.19 and 3.20).

One simple exercise that anyone can try involves taking any object like a salt-shaker and moving it around a table in front of a camera frame by frame. This does require a digital still camera or a digital video camera that is controlled or hooked into a capture software program like Dragonframe or FrameThief. Dragonframe works well with the digital still cameras, and digital video cameras and FrameThief work well together. Mount your camera on a tripod;

Figure 3.20

Setup for the saltshaker experiment.

lock it down with tape or sand bags. Make sure the tripod is on a hard flat surface like a concrete floor. Don't mount your tripod on a rug because the "give"
in the rug could move your camera. Put a simple light on your saltshaker and
start moving it around bit by bit, frame by frame. Shoot two pictures for every
move ("on twos"). Capture about 3 seconds of this. Now, go find a piece of live-
action film of a person who is very nervous or in any other kind of dramatic
emotional state. This reference film should be a QuickTime movie so you can
look at it frame by frame. Notice and analyze how the person moves from
frame to frame. Once you see and understand the action on a single-frame
basis then translate this movement into that saltshaker. Try to be as true to the
reference film as possible and even try exaggerating that movement. If you do
this successfully then you will understand the power of controlled animated
movement in everyday objects. Object animators can elicit a certain kind of
empathy with this quasi-anthropomorphic approach to animation.

If you want to add another layer to this experiment, then try to find a saltshaker that comes in three different sizes. You can substitute the saltshakers
one for the other to get a breathing effect, expanding and contracting.

The Moving Camera

It would be a mistake not to talk about the ability of the camera to be animated.
So far I have stressed the importance of "locking down" your camera so there are
no unnecessary bumps or jarring movements. Yet we did discover that artists
like Blu do intentionally move the camera every frame for certain aesthetic and
often practical reasons. Until recent years, most filmmakers shot in film and the
film cameras were heavy and cumbersome. This was especially true of 35 mm
cameras like the Mitchell that can weigh over 40 pounds.

In order to produce animated shots with camera moves that simulate live-action
camera movements, these heavy Mitchells require large, heavy motion control units

that are controlled by a computer and power drivers. Many of these units are custom-made and many are reproduced, but all are very expensive and difficult to maintain. Some of the lighter units can be used in the field but might not have the accuracy that can be achieved on a hard studio floor with a heavy machine (Figures 3.21 and 3.22).

These days, most filmmakers who work in stop motion and pixilation shoot with DSLR cameras that are small and lightweight. As a result, these large heavy motion-control units are no longer necessary. Newer, more affordable lightweight systems have been constructed from "off-the-shelf" parts. We will explore these in the following chapter about time lapse. The other advantage of these DSLRs is that they can be animated directly with no motion control. In the film *Off-Line*, I took my Nikon D100 and placed it right on my set. By focusing on a particular object in the frame and by utilizing my frame-grabbing capture software, I was able to move the camera through the set in a relatively smooth-moving point-of-view shot. I used "blue tack," a soft putty material, to help hold the camera in place as I shot each frame from the computer. Using the frame comparison tool with your capture software allows you to track images in front of the camera as you move it through an environment and to use those images as guides for smoother animated movements. You need to track the placement of the image or object in front of the camera, remembering to use eases or tight registration on the image. Many capture software programs have markers that you can place on the object/image so that you can see the change from frame to frame.

Figure 3.21

Heavy motion control system for studio shooting. (Courtesy of Mark Roberts Motion Control, Surrey, UK.)

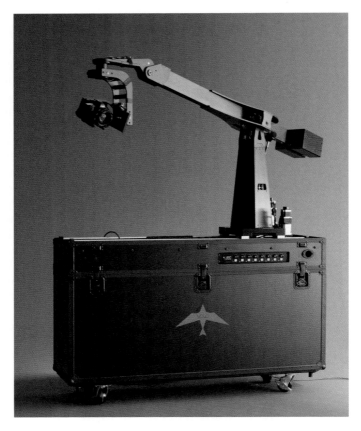

Figure 3.22

Lightweight motion control unit for outdoor shooting. (Courtesy of Jamie Caliri Productions, Ojai, CA.)

These marks are not recorded on the final frames but only act as guidelines. You can even use a simple wooden guide to help control the placement of the camera for each frame. There are many ways to be creative with a camera now that they are small and light, and this kind of filmmaking has become even more accessible to anyone with a good idea and the desire to make a pixilated film and do the work involved (Figure 3.23).

One other fun and relatively simple way to get a moving camera/point-of-view shot is to mount a DSLR camera to the dashboard of your car and take a drive. If you set your shutter to a longer exposure you will get a streaking effect along the sides of the frame but the objects in front of you will not streak or smear quite as much. This can be very effective on a nighttime drive when there are lights everywhere that will streak with a longer exposure such as 1 second. It is critical to make

Figure 3.23

Camera mounted on the set of *Off-Line* by Tom Gasek.

sure that your camera is firmly mounted on the dashboard with tape or some sort of stabilizing base.

By now you can start to see the possibilities and variations using the single-frame camera and the pixilation technique. I am certain that there are some variations that have not been exploited yet, and there many more that I have not mentioned in this chapter. Ultimately, you will need a camera that has single-frame capability, some capture software, a tripod, and most importantly a great idea, and you can start experimenting with this technique, building up a vocabulary of information that will feed into a finished film.

PRO-File Juan Pablo Zaramella

Juan Pablo Zaramella. (Courtesy of Juan Pablo Zaramella.)

JPZ: I first consider myself a filmmaker, then an animator. I've been interested about cinema and animation since I'm conscious. I love to create worlds and unique experiences to the audiences, to transport them to places where they couldn't reach in other ways.

TDG: How long have you been working in stop-motion animation?

JPZ: Around 20 years! I started in animation school, where I discovered that I especially loved to do stop motion.

TDG: How much preproduction did you do before shooting in this technique? Please briefly describe your preproduction approach.

JPZ: The writing and preproduction were held at the same period of time. Writing the story needed to explore the possibilities, so it was a parallel process. Preproduction included a lot of improvisation, where lots of ideas appeared. Then, we thought about how we could construct a story with these ideas. We also had to learn to work with the sunlight, predicting possible changes, considering the changes of speed of the early sun.
My goal was to do a short in which the technique was an inseparable part of the story itself.

TDG: What kind of equipment did you use (i.e., camera, software, lights, post-production software)?

JPZ: We worked with several Canon cameras. The main cameras were a 5D and a 7D. Inside the set, we used a combination of mini pan lights with fluorescent fills. In some interiors, we emulated sunlight using 2k Arri lights.

Shot of Zaramella on the set. (Courtesy of Juan Pablo Zaramella.)

TDG: Do you use motion control? How do you move your camera and with what?

JPZ: No, we decided to do all the camera movements by hand, because we wanted the imperfections in the final result.

TDG: What is it about your approach to stop-motion animation that most appeals to you?

JPZ: One thing that I love about stop motion is that you can recognize the hand of the artist. I don't want perfection. I wanted expression. I'm not against technology. There are wonderful things that you can do with it in stop motion, but in a very advanced digital era, I prefer to put the spotlight on the imperfections when I work in stop motion. For example, when I use Plasticine, I love to see my fingerprints there!

TDG: How closely do you work with a sound track? Please describe your picture/ sound relationship.

JPZ: I love to be part of the conception of the soundtrack! It's half the experience. I usually prepare a reference foley band, using sound banks or recording at home. Then I give it to professionals so they can follow the main idea. I also give them freedom to go ahead with the approach or to propose better things and they do it!

TDG: How important is the movement or animation in your film work?

JPZ: Very important. Being an animator is to have total control over the timing. In animation, you can do exactly what you planned if you like.

TDG: How would you describe the approach to acting in pixilation?

JPZ: I love the experience of working with pixilation for this reason. You can give "cartoon" expression to real actors. And there's a combination of talents: the real "actor" is the mix of the animator and the person that appears in front of camera.

TDG: Do the objects that you use in your stop motion have symbolic meaning? Is it important to see these objects as photographic images versus drawings or computer-generated images?

JPZ: Maybe ... But I usually don't spend a lot of time thinking on concepts or symbols, because in the end I found that it's a limitation for me. Prejudices make you go in very obvious directions. I prefer to give space to my unconscious part, and the symbols appear in the richest way.

Production shot from *Luminaris.* (Courtesy of Juan Pablo Zaramella.)

TDG: Do you think the type of stop motion that you used lends itself to humorous subject matters or can there be a serious approach achieved? What makes this technique humorous or serious?

JPZ: It's difficult to say, because humor and comedy is something that appears in my ideas very spontaneously. Also when I think about serious subjects, comedy emerges in some moments. I don't think that the technique itself is especially good for humor, because this is something that comes from the ideas behind the technique. In my case, I can't escape from this fact.

TDG: Is it important to have an emotional trigger in your work?

JPZ: Yes, absolutely! I try to be emotional, because it makes a stronger connection between the audience and the story.

TDG: Do you use a lot of postproduction work on your stop-motion production or do you like to do all the effects and clean up "in camera"? If you do postproduction what software, edit-ware, or approach do you use?

JPZ: I try to do as many effects in camera as I can, but I use a lot of postproduction anyway. In the digital era, you can save a lot of production time (and money) being conscious about postproduction possibilities.

TDG: How do you market your work? What is the intended audience?

JPZ: I'm not good thinking about audiences or selling. I try to do the movie that I love to see on a screen, hoping that other people would like to see something like this too.

An interior production shot from *Luminaris*. (Courtesy of Juan Pablo Zaramella.)

TDG: Do you have any advice for artists, animators, or novice filmmakers that want to try your methods of using stop motion?

JPZ: Yes: test as much as you can! Try animating the most simple things and characters. If you are able to express with something very simple, you'll express with the most complex character too. The best way to learn is to deal with resources economically.

TDG: Are there any other points that you would like to make regarding your stop-motion work, past or present?

JPZ: I'm thinking now of combining stop motion with other techniques, like live action, CGI, and drawings. It's what I'm working [on] now. My idea is to do a collage with all the techniques, but doing something consistent at the same time. This is my big challenge now! The project is called *Onión*, and it will be ready soon.

4

Time Lapse

Ken Murphy's time-lapse camera setup for *History of the Sky*. (Courtesy of Ken Murphy © 2009.)

Expand Your Awareness
The Intervalometer
Understand Your Subject
Contrast
Shutter Speeds
Time-Lapse Rates and Formulas
Time Lapse and Pixilation
Motion Control

Expand Your Awareness

Time-lapse photography has been practiced for decades and it never seems to grow old. From the early work of Dr. John Ott in the 1930s to the phenomenal motion photography of Ron Fricke in films like *Koyaanisqatsi* to *Baraka* in the 1980s and 1990s, time lapse has allowed us to see the world with a fresh point of view. This technique of stopping the camera and shooting frames at an even and given rate allows viewers to see events sped up in time. It is the complement to slow-motion photography and it reveals the movement in the world around us in a way that we could never experience from straight observation. Ott's early experiments showed the blossoming of flowers and Fricke's work captured the flow of clouds like turbulent water and the flow of human urban movement like blood pulsing in our veins.

Time is often considered the fourth dimension and time-lapse steps into this arena. This kind of stop motion allows us to observe nature in the forms and textures that we understand as natural, since we are using photographic images, but it delivers the added dimension of an expanded view of time. As a result of these properties, scientists have turned to time lapse to help understand our universe and our place in it. Astronomers observe the skies and stars at night using time-lapse sequences. It allows them to see the patterns of movement and development around us. If you go online and view the time-lapse work created from NASA's space station you will be amazed at the beauty and power of this footage. It is informational but it has an aesthetic that's hard to deny (Figure 4.1).

When John Ott started using time lapse, he became fixated on the blossoming of flowers. This observation led him to become an expert on the effects of light, and he has used that information to improve our lives through a better understanding of ultraviolet and infrared rays.

In San Francisco, an experiment took place on the roof of the Exploratorium. Ken Murphy, an artist with a background in electronics, mounted a stationary camera on the roof and captured the moving sky above the building. His project is called *A History of the Sky*. He shot one 1024 × 768 high resolution frame on a digital camera every 10 seconds each day, so one movie is the evolution of that day compressed into a short 6-minute sequence. He then placed all of the movies for each day of the year on monitors next to each other in a grid formation synchronized to the second and it is easy to see the changing patterns of light and weather over a year and how the ebb and flow of these patterns works day to day, season to season. It's both scientific and aesthetic in nature (Figure 4.2).

I've found that *A History of the Sky* elicits a wide range of emotional responses in viewers. By presenting a visual representation of an entire year in just a few minutes, one gets the sense of the fleeting nature of time, which can have a powerful emotional impact.

Ken Murphy

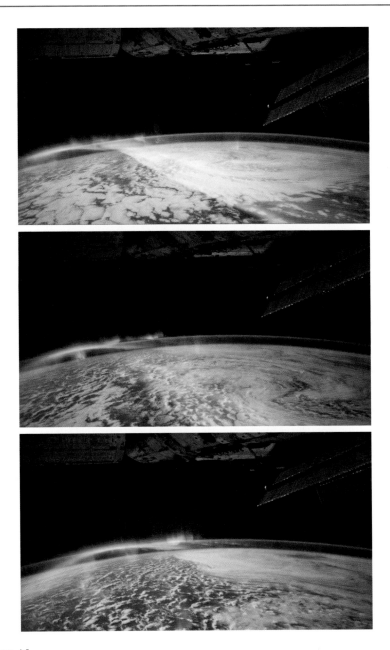

Figure 4.1

Three sequential images of Earth from NASA photographed by Dr. Donald Pettit. (From Space Station Live: Astronaut Don Pettit on Earth Photography, https://www. youtube.com/watch?v=jxcjj4ukpJw.)

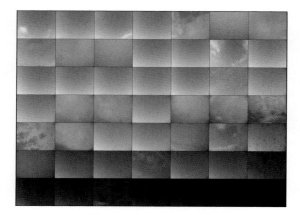

Figure 4.2

A sequence of time-lapse frames from Ken Murphy's *A History of the Sky*. (Courtesy of Ken Murphy © 2009.)

These days there are many filmmakers expanding the capabilities of time lapse and using this frame-by-frame technique as a basis for aesthetic exploration. Geoff Tompkinson, a British-born photographer and filmmaker who lives in Austria, has merged time and motion in his hyperlapse and hyperzoom techniques. Tompkinson has refined a method of moving a DSLR camera, often with a wide lens, through an environment using a time-lapse interval of shooting. He often carries his camera on a handheld rig and carefully plans a route of travel considering where the camera might turn and travel. The camera moves in a free manner that is not possible with a motion-control rig. By carefully shooting and registering objects frame to frame, Tompkinson is able to create footage that is acceptable for the eye to follow. There still is a wild element to the footage, so it is run through postproduction stabilizing with programs like Warp Stabilizer in After Effects. Getting the shooting correct is critical to great final results, so Tompkins does a lot of preproduction:

> The procedure before beginning the shot is to assess the ground conditions and walk the planned route the camera will follow. At this time the idea is to decide which rig I am going to use and to locate pivot points around which the various parts of the move will swing. I also pace out the length of the move to calculate the interframe movement distance required to give me the desired final length of movie. This obviously varies a bit depending on the frame rate being used for the job.
>
> My current Wthrust is in the area of my newly developed technique "HyperZoom™." This technique enables the camera to take a seamless journey around and through a location—or series of locations—without any loss of visual continuity. It's as if the camera is strapped on the back of a flying insect, which can go just about anywhere. I am mainly using this technique with a timelapse approach and often seamlessly mix in Hyperlapse sequences along the route.
>
> **Geoff Tompkinson**

Another contemporary time-lapse film artist, Julian Tryba from New England, uses time lapse combined with postproduction work to attain an effect he calls "layer-lapse." In this technique, he shoots environments (as seen in his Boston layer-lapse film) at different times of the day. With masks, rotoscoping, and mattes, he combines these different times of day and their corresponding light scenarios into one moving image. The effect is magical and is often enhanced by synchronized music, eliciting a unique aesthetic and expanding the possibility of time lapse as an art form (Figures 4.3 and 4.4).

Figure 4.3

Wide shot of Geoff Tompkinson with one of his setups in Dubai. (Courtesy of Geoff Tompkinson.)

Figure 4.4

Layer-lapse of Boston. (Courtesy of Julian Tryba © 2014.)

The Intervalometer

The only way to observe the natural evolution and timing of any event is to record that event at an even rate or interval of shooting. In pixilation, the camera operator can shoot frames at random times depending on what is going on between frames. Pure time lapse must be shot at equal intervals so the regular or irregular timing of an event can be observed. This can be a tedious shooting process unless the shutter of the camera is hooked up to a clock that releases the shutter at a particular rate. This clock is called the "intervalometer." Some digital still cameras like the Nikon and the Canon 7D Mark II have an intervalometer built in, but most require a special remote shutter release component that has the ability to program in time-lapse events. Film cameras also require special intervalometer timers to be attached to them for shutter release capabilities. The other option for digital video or still cameras is to hook them up to capture software programs like Dragonframe, Stop Motion Pro, or FrameThief. They all have intervalometers as an option for shooting (Figure 4.5a–c).

This idea of an expanded awareness of the world around us can easily be demonstrated in the following exercise:

Take a single frame digital still camera and power it from the adapter that you plug into the wall. Hook up the camera to a computer that has a capture software program with an intervalometer (time-lapse) option. Mount the camera high on a tripod over your bed where you sleep at night. Stabilize the camera with sand bags or tape down the tripod to the hard floor. Set the shutter, iris, and focus to manual mode. Have a small night-light in the bedroom that gives off a small amount of light, enough to give the room a low exposure with all the other lights off. Leave this light on as you go to sleep. Set the iris to $f/5.6$ or wider (i.e., $f/2.8$) and adjust the shutter to whatever is required to get a decent exposure with just the night-light on. Just before you go to bed set the intervalometer to shoot every 15 seconds at your optimum exposure. The daylight may overexpose the frame when the morning light

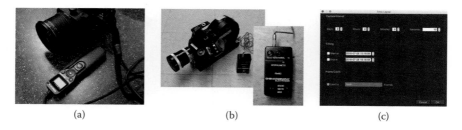

(a) (b) (c)

Figure 4.5

(a) A remote shutter release that has an intervalometer option. (b) A film camera intervalometer that controls its time shutter release. (c) The control panel for the time-lapse option in Dragonframe software.

4. Time Lapse

comes through the window but don't be concerned with this. Set the camera maximum frame count to 2000. If you shoot a frame every 15 seconds that means there will be four frames for every minute of sleep. There will be 60 (60 minutes to an hour) times 4 frames for every hour of sleep (240 frames) and if you sleep 8 hours then you must have 1,920 frames available (8 × 240). You will see what your sleeping habits are and have a greater understanding of a part of your life that you were never aware of. For a little extra fun you can mount a clock near the lens with a small light on it so you can associate your sleeping patterns with a specific time. This is the power of time-lapse.

Understand Your Subject

In order to make a successful time-lapse film, you must first choose an appropriate subject and then study it carefully before shooting the first frame. There are some events that cannot be controlled or predicted, but making initial observations will tell you the length of the event, the extremes of the potential transformation in the event, the way light and exposures will change during the event, and the external conditions that need to be accounted for in order to set a stable camera. There are companies like Harbortronics that build special housing and controls for time-lapse cameras that will allow you to shoot outdoors in most any condition. As Eric Hanson, a veteran effects artist and associate professor at University of Southern California, states:

> We shoot primarily during trips to remote wilderness areas, thus there is some pre-planning using Google Earth and the like, but much is reserved for serendipity, as weather and geography are always an unknown. We did some elaborate pre-planning once when shooting from the lower "Diving Board" of Half Dome in Yosemite Valley, where we wanted to pay homage to Ansel Adam's "Black Monolith" shot. We found the exact time of the terminator shadow sweeping across the face in his shot by writing a script to download time-lapse frames of a webcam of Half Dome, studying it over many months and determining when the best time of year and day would be to shoot. Of course our work is dwarfed by Ansel's, but it was an interesting and fun process.
>
> **Eric Hanson**

There is a wonderful tool that can help you plan the path of the sun when you are scouting out a potential time-lapse location. It's an iPhone application called "Sun Seeker" and it will show you the path of the sun with a superimposed line over any live camera view from your iPhone. It will calculate the path from day to night anytime of the year so you can plan ahead knowing where the sun will be if you scout a location months in advance.

When you choose a subject for time lapse, think about the environments that you go through every day. These are the environments that you understand from constant observation and might make the best subject. You will know where you want to set the camera, what occurs during any period of time, and where any movement is concentrated. It is important to have dramatic transformation in the environment or to find an action that is too slow to perceive without time-lapse.

The dramatic transformation will make for an interesting sequence, and the slow action or transformation sped up with time lapse will be fascinating to see and potentially revealing from an observational point of view.

Contrast

When viewing a piece of time-lapse photography it is helpful to show contrast within the frame. This use of contrast always makes any compositional frame interesting but it is critical for time lapse. Since time-lapse speeds actions up, the overall frame becomes highly active. If there are no stationary elements in the frame to help set off the action then the action becomes a blur of activity and your audience will lose focus. This kind of contrast can be easily achieved by careful compositional design. If you are shooting people outdoors in a city then it's important to place some stationary buildings within the frame. The people, cars, and shadows from the moving sun or artificial light will move around the solid immobile building and the eye of the viewer will be able to focus on the activity and rest on the stationary elements. It's important to know how the shadows and key source of light will shift or whether you might get a light flare. All of this will add to the active frame, so making sure there are some stationary elements helps as a stable visual reference in a highly active frame (Figure 4.6).

In any moving image, it usually is the active element in the image that draws our eye. If we view a static still frame and suddenly an eye blinks or a distant

Figure 4.6

Shot of streaking people walking through a doorframe.

plane jets across the composition, then that is what we look at. Time lapse is no different but the opposite can be true in time lapse and pixilation. When a frame is loaded with activity the eye tends to be drawn to the less active object or area. It's this contrast that can be used to direct the viewer and highlight a particular action that you want to feature in any shot.

When camera movement is combined with time lapse, then the contrast or stable elements in the frame will change. Often what filmmakers like Geoff Tompkinson do with the hyperlapse is to focus on one particular image and make it the focal point of the frame. Pushing in on a particular location or person and then setting a new focus point is how the moving camera operates. The focal point does change as the camera continues to move through a scene but there is always enough time to register the image before moving on to the next point. Ultimately, the filmmaker wants to keep the viewer engaged and able to follow along without losing visual landmarks. Time lapse speeds movement up, so it is important to keep the image fluid in its movement and focused and then refocused on particular images.

Shutter Speeds

One follow-up to the subject of contrast can be found in the simple adjustment of the shutter speed in your camera. We have already made a point of the critical element of having manual shutter, iris, and focus control in your stop-motion camera work. You are the one in control, not the camera. Since the majority of stop-motion camera work takes place from a tripod or stabilized motion control unit, any shutter speed is possible to use. Any handheld camera work requires a fast shutter speed (a quarter second or faster) to avoid soft focus or movement during the exposure. If the camera is moving while the shutter is open then the frame will smear or elicit a soft focus effect. Stop motion by hand is a rare event even for an artist like Blu, who is constantly changing the angle of his camera frame to frame. He shoots from a tripod so the camera is steady during the exposure and the focus is clear. Since we are on a tripod, the shutter speed can be quite long because the camera is stable. Any movement in front of a long shutter exposure will smear across the frame and anything that doesn't move will remain sharp and in focus. This is the same principle that we used in light painting. So if you want to heighten the contrast in your time-lapse photography, then shoot at longer shutter speeds on a tripod. The moving images will streak and the stable images will remain focused, giving the contrast that you need. The longer the shutter speed, the longer the streak effect, especially when shooting lights. This will have the effect of smoothing out the action in contrast to the more staccato appearance of most stop-motion images, which are sharp and unblurred frame to frame. You will have to close your iris down for the longer shutter exposure in daylight or use a neutral density (ND) filter or a filter called the Big Stopper by Lee Filters to darken the image. You will have to open up the iris for night events in order to maintain a good overall exposure in the dark (Figure 4.7a–c).

(a)	(b)	(c)

Figure 4.7

(a) Night city scene with a shutter exposure of 1/2 second. (b) Night scene with a shutter speed of 1 second. (c) Night scene with a shutter speed of 5 seconds.

Time-Lapse Rates and Formulas

Determining the rate of the interval for a particular event may take some experimentation. This is why it is important to know how long an event occurs, like the rising of the moon. How long do you let time lapse before you shoot another frame? The moon may take many hours to rise and if you want to highlight the dramatic rise of the moon, then speeding up that progression will be more effective. That means that you want to allow more time to lapse between frames, giving the moon a chance to rise between shots. If you are photographing people then you may not want to have too much time between shots. People move relatively fast (certainly in comparison to the moon). It may take a person 4–5 seconds to walk across a large room, so if you shoot a frame every 2 seconds then you will only get two frames for that action. That's not enough to get a sense of the movement or direction of the action. You may want to consider shooting a frame every half second so you end up with 10 frames for that action. This way you can see the action and direction in what will play out as less than a half second of screen time. Since the moon is so slow you may consider a longer lapse, more in the 15- to 30-second range, so the change can be perceived in a dramatic playback. It's important to consider what the main focus of your time lapse is and set the interval accordingly. If you want to watch the sun rise at a good steady rate then your interval will be longer, but you will have clouds that streak by at a fast pace. If the clouds are your main focus then the interval will be faster and the sun will not rise that fast in the sky.

If there are restrictions on the length of the playback and you need to squeeze a time-lapse event into that length then there is a formula to help figure out the interval between shots.

If, through observation, you have determined that the event that you want to make a time-lapse film of is 3 hours long and you have to compress those 3 hours into a 15-second piece of film then you can work out the interval of the shutter exposure through simple math.

4. Time Lapse

H = length of event in hours
S = length of time lapse in seconds
F = frame rate
I = interval rate

$$60 \times (H \times 60) / (S \times F) = I$$
$$60 \times (3 \times 60) / (15 \times 30) = 24$$

So in order to shoot a 3-hour event in time lapse with a playback frame rate of 30 frames per second in 15 seconds of playback time, you must shoot a frame every 24 seconds.

Time Lapse and Pixilation

We noted earlier that it was difficult to be the person behind and in front of the camera simultaneously when creating a pixilated film. One way to accomplish this approach is to use time lapse while animating yourself or other people in front of the camera. This is not an easy task and takes a lot of concentration, but here's an exercise that will allow you to try this out for yourself:

This exercise will test your knowledge of the animation principles of easing, momentum, and secondary motion. Contrast is another element that we discussed and it is integral to the success of this exercise. First you must take your camera on a tripod and place it in an area where there is a high level of human activity, like a busy downtown street or a university campus. Be aware that anytime you shoot pictures in public you must obey any posted notices that would prevent you from photographing people. You will find these notices in subways, airports, hospitals, and other such places. If your camera does not have an intervalometer built into it then you must bring a laptop computer with a capture software program that has the time-lapse option, or if you're using a DSLR camera consider buying and using a remote cable connection that has an intervalometer built into it. Set your time-lapse interval to 3 seconds and make sure that the sound option is on so you can hear a click every time a picture is taken. Make sure you have enough frames on your flash card if you don't have a computer, or make sure your total amount of frames to take is above 1,000 on your computer. Set up a place for you to be in the frame that is stable and supported, like a chair, at a table, or against a wall. You are going to move increment by increment every 3 seconds (as the camera shoots). You will be holding your position for extended periods, and this can be physically challenging; thus having some support will help. This requires moving extremely slowly or actually posing bit by bit every 3 seconds, including your eases and normal animation principles. Shoot for about an hour and then stop. When you play back your film, you will appear to be moving in a more normal pace as the world frantically zips by you. The contrast draws our eye to your slower action, and you have had a chance to practice some animation as the actual animated subject.

Motion Control

We touched on the moving camera in Chapter 3, where I mentioned that a whole new world of motion control is now available. Again, because of the lightweight quality of DSLR cameras, the heavy expensive machines of the past have become dinosaurs. Artists and designers like Chris Church, who created Dynamic Perception, are sharing their information about off-the-shelf hardware and common-use software that is available to anyone who has the time, patience, and curiosity to explore. Chris has an open-source site called openmoco.org, where contributors and viewers share experiences, resources, software, and reviews to help you build your own system. Steel and aluminum rails are bought off the shelf or can be custom-made to specification and there are "astronomical" mounts that are placed on the rails for pan/tilt capability. All of this is run by Arduino circuit boards. According to their site (available at https://www.arduino.cc/):

> Arduino is an open-source electronics prototyping platform based on flexible, easy-to-use hardware and software. It's intended for artists, designers, hobbyists, and anyone interested in creating interactive objects or environments.

Now, you may think "this is beyond my capability," but you might be surprised and find some already fabricated hardware and software setups (Figure 4.8).

Camera motion is not absolutely critical to making a successful time-lapse film, but it certainly is what the experts are using for greater depth perception and it adds a whole other quality and control to the output. You can create your own camera rigs with guides, rails (wood or metal), and with geared heads mounted on the track. This all must be controlled by hand, but it takes some very exacting, demanding concentration and work to add this element. Camera movement should not be used just for the sake of movement. Take advantage of the changing perspective that a camera move might offer. A camera move might reveal new and important visual information. Constant use of camera move-ment starts to become tedious and the lack of contrast in shots can diminish your film. Use these techniques sparingly and create an interesting dynamic in your filmmaking.

Figure 4.8

A rail and track setup from Eric Hanson. (Courtesy of Eric Hanson © 2010.)

4. Time Lapse

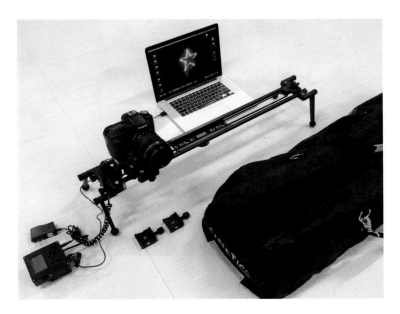

Figure 4.9

Cinetics Axis360 portable rail and pan tilt head for motion control.

The more advanced capture software programs like Dragonframe also have controls for motion control hardware. You can check the capture software's website to see what cameras and off-the-shelf motion control hardware are compatible with the driver-controlled software. Here is an example of a system that works with Dragonframe made by Cinetics (Figure 4.9).

One camera that many sports and outdoor camera people use is the GoPro. This is a high-definition video camera that has single-frame capability. The camera bodies are very small and the company has created various types of housing and mounts that allow the filmmaker to capture unusual point-of-view shots (i.e., skiing downhill, swimming underwater, and many more). These cameras have some settings but are primarily automatic. This presents some problems for stop motion since the images could vary in exposure frame to frame in traditional stop-motion capturing. Some companies are starting to adapt the GoPro to include C-mount changeable lenses and iris "lock-in," which can help stop-motion filmmakers. At the moment, there are no straightforward stop-motion capture software programs that work easily with GoPro but, as we know, capture software is not always necessary for all of these single frame stop-motion techniques. Time lapse is one of those techniques that is suited for the GoPro. The built-in wide lens, interval controls (intervalometer), and automatic settings can work because of the constant shooting execution. Any change in exposure will seem natural and probably gradual and not jarring. It will be

Figure 4.10

Tom Lowe shooting time lapse in Manzanar at night. (Courtesy of Tom Lowe and Timescapes.org © 2010.)

very interesting to see how these cameras adapt to market demand and remain unique, compact, and effective.

The final word on time lapse in this chapter should be given to Tom Lowe, who is a time lapse master and creator of timescapes.org. There is a time-lapse forum on his site that has an incredibly in-depth conversation about the state of time-lapse today. Lowe produced a feature film utilizing time-lapse photography and trailers, and many of his shots can be viewed and shared on his site (Figure 4.10).

> I have no background in photography or filmmaking at all. I'm just totally self-taught, by trial and error. Back when I started, I had nowhere I could ask questions, no one to seek advice from. I felt like I was re-inventing the wheel with every small step of progress. This was the main impetus for me to start the Timescapes.org time-lapse discussion forum. Today, we have over *7000* members sharing advice and techniques related to time-lapse. This is a great resource for beginners, because it allows them to skip all the painful trial and error to a large degree!
>
> **Tom Lowe**

4. Time Lapse

5

Cinematography, Lighting, and Composition

Close-up of a camera lens with animated squash and stretch sequence super-imposed on lens. (Courtesy of Tom Gasek © 2011.)

Cameras and Lenses
Camera Controls
Animated Lighting
Compositional Beginnings and Ends

Cameras and Lenses

We have already established that at the moment of this writing DSLR still cameras are the standard for shooting alternative, non-puppet, photographic stop-motion techniques. Their light weight and small size offer convenience and quality in the shooting environment. They are relatively affordable with prices that range from $400 to $9000, with the average price around $1500 for a high quality "prosumer" camera. Although Canon and Nikon are leaders in this area, many of the other brands like Olympus, Pentax, Leica, Ricoh, and Sony offer equally effective products. There are some features that are better on some cameras over others. The critical feature, which we have already touched on, is that the camera must have manual shutter, iris, focus, and white balance options. These options should be available by switching a control on the camera and not by having to constantly hold down a particular control to achieve this effect. Another important feature that is not absolutely critical to have but a great option for these cameras is the live view mode. This will allow you to hook up your DSLR to a computer with stop-motion software and see a live image from the camera. The ability to compare live and previously captured frames through live view makes this option a real plus. Advanced stop-motion capture programs like Dragonframe and Stop Motion Pro pick up live view if your camera has this feature, which is included in most new cameras. This will make your life much easier. The only other options are to hook up a small digital camera to your viewfinder or set up a digital camera that is operated at a parallax point of view or along the side of your DSLR (Figure 5.1).

The reason manual controls are critical is because the images that move in front of the camera vary in color and light reflectance depending on how dominant they are in the frame. An automatic camera is programmed to constantly adjust and average for the best exposure for each individual frame. This is very convenient for still photography, where each photograph exists

Figure 5.1

The camera on the left is a video tap, and the camera on the right has live view built in.

5. Cinematography, Lighting, and Composition

on its own when it is viewed. In animation, we often look at hundreds of images together and if the automatic exposures are constantly changing from one frame to the next, as the imagery changes in front of the camera, then there will be wild fluctuations in the exposure as a movie plays. This is highly distracting. Controlling the exposure, white balance, focus, and image stabilizer and locking them in with a manual setting will greatly reduce this fluctuation.

There is another reason that exposure fluctuation can occur. That is because most digital still cameras come with automated lenses. When an iris is set on a camera, in manual or automatic mode, the iris shuts down to that f-stop when the shutter exposes and then opens back up so the viewer can see through the viewfinder. The open iris allows more light in for better viewing or a live view image. If an animator is shooting hundreds of frames, there can be a slight variation in the iris aperture when it shuts down and opens up over those numerous frames, and that can account for the slightly varying exposures. There are a couple of solutions to this issue. One is to use a manual lens that doesn't have the capability to open and close for viewing every frame but stays in its set position all the time. This may require a camera that allows you to change the lens. If your shutter is set at a higher number f-stop, shutting down the iris, then you might not get a very bright live view image. This can be a bit problematic. I usually shoot around 4 to 5.6 when I use my manual lenses. Another solution, not recommended, is filing down the pin in the lens that triggers this action in an automatic lens. Some camera operators use tape to hold down the pin on the back of the lens that engages these automatic functions. These are not elegant solutions but are practiced in the field. One advantage to using a Canon camera with Nikon lenses is that the adaptor that allows the Nikon lens to work with the Canon camera depresses that control pin, eliminating any unwanted functions. Finally, there are postproduction solutions to help reduce this fluttering. We'll get into this last option later in this book (Figure 5.2).

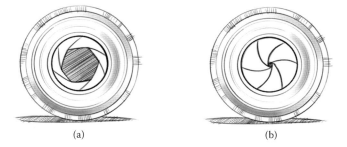

(a)   (b)

Figure 5.2

Sketch of two irises, (a) open and (b) semi-closed.

There is always a preference for "prime" lenses, which are single focal range lenses. They have less glass in the lens, theoretically making for sharper images with less distortion. Prime lenses are usually lighter in weight and often have a larger open aperture, which is great for shooting in low light situations. Zoom lenses, which often come with new cameras, are quite well made these days. Their image quality is excellent. They also have a larger set of options for focal range for the price of the matching prime lenses. Having a set of prime lenses, including 18, 24, 35, 55, 85, and 105 mm/macro, will give you everything you should need for making a successful film, but if you can't afford that then a zoom that ranges from 18 to 135 mm should work quite well. If you buy into a certain brand of lens and then decide to use another brand of camera, there are lens adapters so you can mix and match. Many professionals these days are using Canon cameras and Nikon lenses but there are other combinations that work as well. Canon, Nikon, and Carl Zeiss are considered excellent brands for lenses, but as usual there are many more (Figure 5.3).

One technique that the manual lens allows the cinematographer to practice is the "rack focus." This is a classic live-action effect that allows the filmmaker to direct the eye of the viewer from one object or person to another object or person when they are separated by depth in the frame within a composition. A foreground element can be in focus and a background element will be soft in focus. The story suddenly requires the background element to be seen so the camera lens can be shifted to move the focus and attention from the front to the back of the compositional frame. This is usually executed by using a gentle ease-in and accelerated turns of the focus ring on the lens, including an ease-out over a short number of frames (i.e. 10–20 frames). This can be done by hand with a measuring device on the lens (like a piece of tape with marked increments) or it can be achieved through a motion-control setup. Depth of field is an important element to consider when shooting with a DSLR camera. The basic principle is that the lower the number on the f-stop (i.e., $f/1.4$, $f/2.8$, etc.), the more narrow the depth of field or range of the focus. The audience will automatically look at focused objects in a composition because we seek information that we can understand. That is why the rack focus or

Figure 5.3

A shot of a lens adapter (Nikon lens/Canon camera).

shifting focus is so effective in directing the viewer. The narrow focus also allows the focused object in the frame to stand out in contrast to its soft focused surroundings. If you have a relatively busy background that you don't have control over, then you might consider opening up the iris to create a shallow depth of field to help your subject stand out from the background. The danger with this is that if your subject is moving in the z-axis, or toward and away from the camera, then that subject may fall out of focus in the action. It is also worth noting that every lens has a different range of focus. The wider the lens, like 14–35 mm, the deeper the range of focus or depth of field. Longer lens and macro (or close-up) lenses have a much narrower depth of field. So a 24-mm lens at $f/8$ will have a broader depth of field than an 85-mm lens at $f/8$. Using this knowledge can increase your sense of composition, narrative, and atmospheric quality and is one more tool to give your film a sense of style and purpose. If you view any of the films of the Brothers Quay, like the 1986 *Street of Crocodiles*, you will see a mastery of this use of depth of field (Figure 5.4).

Another type of lens I want to mention is the "tilt–shift" lens. The tilt–shift lens, made by most of these companies, is highly sophisticated in design and as a result is very expensive. This concept has been around for a while in copy camera equipment or with bellows cameras. Basically, the lenses can be tilted so the glass of the lens is not parallel to the film or image sensor plane. This changes the plane of focus, which can be highly, effective especially with a shallow depth of field (Figures 5.5 and 5.6).

This effect has had a comeback recently and can be seen in still photography as well as pixilation or time lapse. Because there is this tilt of the lens and focal plane, the effect almost mimics the effect of a macro lens that is used on very small subjects and that has a shallow depth of field. Life-scale images like people, building, cars, or anything that you shoot with this effect looks like a miniature. This is especially true if the camera is placed above the subject, further enhancing the illusion of a miniature. One of the most successful practitioners of this approach is Keith Loutit. On his website you can see the strange worlds that he creates from real environments, transforming them into toy-like worlds using the tilt lens and speeding up the action through time-lapse photography.

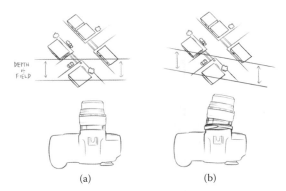

(a)   (b)

Figure 5.5

Diagram of a camera lens with a normal, parallel depth of field (a) and a camera lens with a diagonal depth of field that corresponds to the angle of the tilted lens (b).

Figure 5.6

Examples of the tilt focus effect from Monica Garrison. (Courtesy of Monica Garrison © 2010.)

The "shift" in tilt–shift refers to when the lens plane is moved up and down or side to side and that movement is parallel to the image plane. This allows tall or wide objects to be photographed without tilting the camera and lens (which normally forces diverging perspective lines in the object). Architects often use this technique in order to get straight and undistorted photographs of buildings. This effect is not used as much as the tilt effect, which can also be simulated in postproduction in programs like Photoshop and After Effects with more control (Figure 5.7).

The technology of digital cameras and devices is continuing to expand. A few years back Aardman Animations had a team of creatives use a Nokia N8 cell phone with the capability to shoot high definition video and stills through its Carl Zeiss lens. The team attached a custom cell scope with an adjustable depth of field, which is basically a microscope, to the Nokia N8 and they animated tiny natural objects and models the size of a pencil lead created through 3D printing (Figure 5.8).

Aardman's directing team, called *Sumo Science*, also produced a very large stop-motion animated short film on a beach in Wales using sand, water, a boat,

Figure 5.7

Shot of a camera with the tilt adjusted in a tilt–shift lens setup.

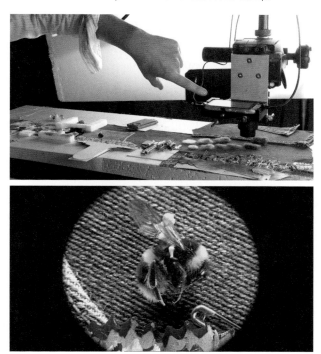

Figure 5.8

The Making of Dot, the world's smallest character animation. (Courtesy of Aardman Animations, Bristol, UK.)

Figure 5.9

The Aardman Animations directorial team, SUMO SCIENCE, consisting of Ed Patterson and Will Studd. (Courtesy of Aardman © 2010.)

and a man dressed in a fisherman's outfit (Figure 5.9). This short is titled *Gulp* and was also shot on a Nokia N8 camera phone.

Camera Controls

When I first started using digital still cameras about 15 years ago I knew very little about the way they worked. I certainly understood film camera technology and soon discovered that digital still camera technology is based on film technology. Even though there is no film involved, the principles are the same. There is a sensor chip instead of film, but the 45-degree mirror that sends the image to the viewfinder and shuts out the light from the film/chip plane when it is not being exposed is the same. This is why they call it the "single-lens reflex" camera. Some newer technologies are eliminating the mirror all together. I ordered about seven different cameras, tested them, and returned all but one for my shoot. What I learned was that all of the cameras operate in the same basic way, so once you learn how one works then the rest are easy to figure out.

One of the newer technologies is the micro four-thirds camera, which has eliminated the mirror in the camera housing and allows for a constant monitoring of the image without having to set up the live view feature. The *m43* refers to the size of the image sensor inside of the camera. These cameras are lightweight, eliminating the mirror, and the lenses are smaller and often less expensive, but this is not necessarily the best option for stop-motion animators. If you are looking to save money on a camera, then webcams might be an option. Remember that having manual controls is a very important part of capturing successful

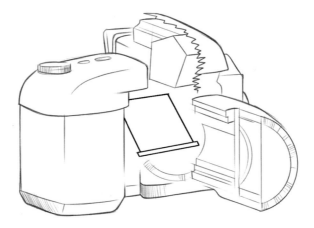

Figure 5.10

Diagram of the 45-degree mirror on the single-lens reflex camera.

frame-by-frame images. Go to the capture software websites to see recommendations for compatible webcams and other cameras (Figure 5.10).

All DSLR cameras work with batteries and/or a power adapter option. Usually when you buy a camera the power adapter does not come with the camera. You will get a battery and battery charger. You might have to buy the power adapter separately. I feel that this is a worthwhile investment. Many of these frame-by-frame techniques require shooting in locations that are not near power sources so the batteries are critical to operating the camera. The risk is, of course, that the camera might run out of power before a shot is complete. Yes, you can change the battery in midshot *if* you have a spare charged battery on hand and *if* you can get to the battery without disturbing the camera. The issue is that you may risk bumping the locked-down camera in midshot, compromising your image stability. You might potentially get a color shift in the digital camera once you change the battery (although this can be corrected in post because these shifts are usually minimal). Many cameras have their batteries located on the bottom of the camera body, and if you have mounted your camera on a tripod or a solid flat surface then you may have to move the camera to change out the battery. Ultimately, using a power adapter from the beginning of each shot will eliminate this problem and will allow you to shoot for longer periods of time uninterrupted (Figure 5.11).

The settings for manual controls are easy to find. A dial for the iris and shutter changes will be located on an area near the read-out panel, usually found on top of the camera. There may be a switch along the side of the lens to put it in manual focus mode. You also want to make sure to turn off the image stabilizer along the side of the lens. This can cause trouble in some compression modes and it is not necessary with a locked-down camera on a tripod. You will have to spend a little time with the camera to understand how it works, but that time is well worth it.

Figure 5.11

A shot of the camera with open bottom, the battery, power adapter, and charger.

There will be a menu button on the back that will allow you to program your camera. There are many features that will be offered in this area, including viewing options, white balance, formatting (erasing all of your images on the camera), image/file sizes, and much more. The image size of your picture is an important choice. New cameras usually have three different file types, corresponding to different sizes: JPEG, TIFF, and what is known as *raw*. The raw image is all the information that the image sensor is able to give you with no compression; this file type gives you the most capabilities for image manipulation in postproduction. The raw file size varies from camera to camera. This is the best quality image, much bigger in size than you would need for high definition playback (which is 1920 pixels wide and 1080 pixels high). Shooting JPEG files (high or medium quality) will give you plenty of image to work with later on. It is great having nice-looking images and you will have the capability to enlarge these raw images and create more detailed postwork on these images because of the added data information. The great advantage to raw images is that they carry a lot more metadata on each image so if you happen to have the wrong color balance setting during a shoot you can still correct it in postproduction color correction. This is much more difficult with the JPEG compression. There is one drawback to using these kinds of larger raw picture files.

That drawback has to do with the time it takes for larger files to be processed in the camera. It can take from 1 to 15 seconds to allow each frame to be processed and placed on the flash card or computer control system, depending on how old your camera and flash card are. Now, 15 seconds doesn't seem long, but when you are animating a person holding unusual and demanding positions then that

15 seconds multiplied by several hundred shots can make all the difference in the successful completion of a shot. If you are shooting objects that can remain stable and unmoving between shots, then the digital still camera processing issue is not a problem, except it may slightly throw off the rhythm of the animator. Humans are not immobile objects. The larger the file format, the longer it takes to process each frame. It's at this point that you want to consider what kind of file size to use when animating humans or anything that requires a faster shooting pace. The newer compact flash cards like the Lexar 300× series have greatly improved this lag time and are often a little more expensive but worth the price. This technology is improving every day and most of the brand new DSLR cameras can capture one frame per second continuously. Digital video cameras capture frames much faster and allow for a faster shooting pace than digital still cameras because the frames are small in size. High definition frames will take longer than standard definition frames, but that is rapidly changing. Standard definition frames can look great if you have a good camera. It can be projected well with a good system, but you cannot enlarge those frames very much and any postproduction work will not be as accurate as working with a file with more data and definition. The high definition files will eventually put all standard definition images to rest.

One final note regarding DSLR cameras has to do with the basic maintenance of these sensitive pieces of equipment. Dirt, lint, and all sorts of fine particles can get into your camera and sit on the low-pass filter in front of your image sensor. Sometimes static electricity makes this happen. Changing lenses is the main way that dust can get onto the filter and sensor. Try to keep lens changes to a minimum and change only in a clean interior room. If you need to change lenses on location or outside, try to do it inside a car or out of the wind to avoid wind-blown particles entering the camera. There are ways that you can clean the filter, but it is very delicate work. Many of the newer prosumer grade cameras have ultrasonic auto-sensor-cleaning as an option. But often the dirt has to be swabbed out by hand. Most DSLR cameras have a sensor-cleaning mode, which requires you to lift and hold the mirror open, revealing the low-pass filter in front of the sensor. This can be carefully cleaned with a proper swab like the sensor wand and proper cleaning fluid, which you can get at a photographic store. There is also antistatic pressured air that you can blow on the filter to remove dirt. You might seriously consider having a reputable camera store clean your image sensor. Cleaning it yourself can result in a scratch on the low-pass filter and it will be costly to replace.

These cameras were made for single-frame shooting and not really for moviemaking or multihour use of multiframe exposures. Sensors can also overheat when they are in live view for long periods of time. So the cameras get what I call "pixel burnout" (also referred to as "hot pixels" or "stuck pixels"). This is usually apparent when shooting into a darker compositional field or during long exposures. When you throw the individual picture files onto a large screen, you can see bright little spots that are the burnt pixels. Blue seems to be the first color that appears in these pixels. Eventually you will have to have your

Figure 5.12

Shot of an open camera with the mirror in place and with the mirror lifted to expose the low-pass filter.

Figure 5.13

An example of dirt on the image sensor low-pass filter and an example of pixel burnout.

image sensor replaced, but in the meantime there are postproduction solutions like pixel sampling. This basically assigns the burnt-out bright pixel to be replaced with the color of the pixel next to it in postproduction.

Burnt pixels and dust on the sensor or low-pass filter are especially noticeable on moving shots. They are also much more difficult to clean up on a moving camera shot over locked-down shots. It is better to address the issue (of potentially replacing the sensor) than trying to fix each problem in postproduction. You should include sensor cleaning as a standard part of your camera maintenance plan (Figures 5.12 and 5.13).

Animated Lighting

Lighting is a real strength in photographic animation. One of the worst mistakes to make in any stop-motion technique is to light an image with flat, overall lighting. Lighting should give form, dimension, atmosphere, drama, and life to any object

5. Cinematography, Lighting, and Composition

or person. Selective lighting can make a stop-motion animation feel larger, adding mystery and drama. Side or under-lighting can add tension and weight. This is a huge area to explore and experiment in, but it is important to understand the basics first. The simple formula for basic lighting is to use key, rim, and fill lighting to get the best result. This is known as "three-point lighting" (Figure 5.14).

Simplicity can also be very effective. Single-source studio lighting has a very dramatic look, and you're only using one light (Figure 5.15).

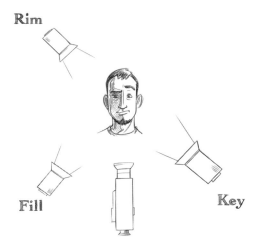

Figure 5.14

A drawn diagram of the key, rim, and fill three-point lighting setup.

Figure 5.15

An example of single-source lighting with no bounce card.

There are all sorts of lighting combinations, but trying to maintain one main shadow with a key light is the best place to start. When you light a person or object, start with the key and see what it lights. Then start building with rims or fill, turning each light on and off to see if you really need it and what its effect is on the person or object. The use of reflector boards and foam core can be very effective as fill light and can be illuminated from the spill of a key light. These lighting techniques have been simulated in painting for centuries. "Sfumato" is the technique of blending colors with similar mid-tones and creating gentle gradients of color and light, and "chiaroscuro" is the much more dramatic use of single-source lighting that creates high contrasting lights and darks. Leonardo da Vinci was a master of the former and Rembrandt mastered the latter.

Moving or animating the lights in a shot is another element to consider when preparing your preproduction. We have moved light sources with the light painting technique discussed earlier. You can also move lights on stands frame by frame with guides for smoother effects. Use your software capture program to gauge the light movement. Professionals often use computer-operated motion control to move lights around a set. It is virtually impossible to achieve the same lighting effect in postproduction. Rheostats, autotransformers, or dimmers are another way to fade lights in and out of shots. If you are turning lights on and off constantly then consider using dimmers to help extend the life of the bulbs. Switching bulbs on and off can be very hard on the filaments in the bulb and thus they burn out a lot faster. Dragonframe software has integrated DMX lighting, which allows for lighting control through a DMX controller box. An animator can connect lighting changes to specific frames and sequences of frames along with other types of controls like "front light/back light," a matting technique that requires two different sets of lighting scenarios. This is usually used in a controlled studio situation due to the use of the computer and DMX box (Figures 5.16 and 5.17).

What size lights should you use? Generally, the same rules that apply for live-action lighting apply to stop motion *but* on a smaller scale. Instead of using a 650-watt bulb for a key light, you might consider a 150-watt bulb. Most stop motion is on a smaller scale, so over-lighting can be a problem. The only real exception might be shooting that is done in the studio with pixilation of people or additional lighting needed for "out in the field." Since the subject matter is larger, you will need to cover more ground. It's logical. Lamps that have fresnel lenses for focusing and softening the light are very helpful. There are many brands, but it is not necessary to pay high prices for these lamps. You can find lamp housing with barn doors that are used for stage lighting and the cost will be less than the traditional movie lighting brands. Light-emitting diodes (LEDs) are another wonderful, if slightly expensive, alternative to miniature lighting of objects. They are bright, often colored, cool in temperature, and highly efficient. It is possible to find LED lights at a less expensive price by shopping at DIY-type shopping warehouses. The LEDs that are sold in film and camera stores seem to carry a premium price, but there are far less expensive LEDs that are equally effective for a fraction of the price. These might have to be adapted a bit with the use of materials like "black wrap" or foil.

Figure 5.16

Shot of a professional autotransformer.

DMX LIGHTING *DDMX-S2*

ABOUT THE DDMX-S2

The DDMX-S2 is a hardware device that you can pair with Dragonframe to:

- Automate a work light (bash light) turning on and off.
- Automate front-light/back-light lighting passes.
- Automate keyframe-based lighting programs for your scene.
- Trigger a RED camera, film camera, or unsupported still camera.
- Trigger a motion-control system for shoot-move-shoot integration.
- Trigger Dragonframe from an external system.

CONTROL LIGHTING

DMX512 (or DMX) is a standard protocol for controlling lighting. When paired with one or more DMX dimmer/switch packs, you can control up to 99 different light channels.

CONTROL DEVICES

Interact with external devices using the built-in relay switch, digital input and digital output.

WHAT ELSE DO I NEED?

The DDMX-S2 interfaces Dragonframe to one or more DMX dimmer/switch packs. You will need to buy a DMX dimmer/switch pack in order to power your lights. You can find several **DMX dimmer packs** at Amazon.com. Make sure that the one you choose can handle the power requirements of your lights. You will also need a DMX cable. You should not use a microphone cable, but a **true DMX cable**. If you use a 5-pin DMX dimmer pack, you will need a **5-pin to 3-pin adapter**.

Figure 5.17

Shot of a DMX box off of the Dragonframe site.

Animated Lighting

Even the proper use of flags can give you the control you might need in a controlled object animation studio shoot (Figure 5.18).

The color temperature of lights used to be an issue when shooting film because the film labs would develop the film based on daylight temperatures. If your lights were warmer than 3200 foot-candles (the lighting measurement standard for daylight), then the film would come out yellow and red. Now when you shoot a DSLR camera with any light you can see the final image immediately and you can adjust any number of controls, like white balance (in manual mode), to correct for the color imbalance. There is also the postproduction color correction option (especially if you have raw files) (Figure 5.19).

Figure 5.18

Shot of consumer LED lights bought at a DIY shop for home goods.

Figure 5.19

Several small 150-watt lamps with barn doors and Fresnel lenses.

5. Cinematography, Lighting, and Composition

Finally, I want to mention indoor and outdoor lighting and the effects of shadows. Indoor shooting has much more control because you are the one setting the lights. Outside, the "big" key light in the sky, otherwise known as "the sun," is in control. If your shadows are too dark on an inside shoot, then you need to add fill light for a bit of definition on the subject. The shadows will be stable or will only move when your animated subject moves, but outside the story is different. Since the Earth is constantly moving, the relationship to the sun changes and shadows will move in an even fashion. We can see this quite clearly in an extended piece of time-lapse photography outdoors. Exterior fill lights will have to move or shooting times will have to be very short. So if you are shooting pixilation outdoors, then you want to think about the rate of shooting that you need to maintain in order to have even shadow movement. Erratic shadow movement can be very distracting unless it is part of the overall effect.

Compositional Beginnings and Ends

Like time lapse, any of these stop-motion techniques can use camera movement to enhance a shot. We explored motion control, geared heads, and even moving the camera itself by hand with a guide. The important point to keep in mind is the beginning and end positions of your camera and the continuously changing composition. It is absolutely critical to practice a run-through of the movement before you commit to shooting frames. In more traditional puppet stop motion, animators perform what is known as a "pop-through." This is a run-through of the shot that records camera and subject movement every 4–10 frames. Any issues that arise will be revealed with the changing lights, shadows, focus, and other difficulties that you will encounter. Once you have addressed these problems, you can adjust for them, and the choreography of your shot will flow smoothly. Know where you are going so the camera and subject matter can stay in sync. This is the equivalent of the cue mark for live-action actors.

One wonderful resource to consider is Joseph Mascelli's *The Five C's of Cinematography: Motion Picture Filming Techniques*. Camera angles, continuity, cutting, close-ups, and composition are all important elements to any film production including frame-by-frame animation. Many consider this text a classic for filmmakers. The next area that we need to investigate is the actual subject that will be animated. What or who will be put in front of the camera and manipulated in a slow and arduous process? Are there any ways to make this work any easier or does the expression "no pain, no gain" apply? This is what we'll explore next.

6

Objects, People, and Places

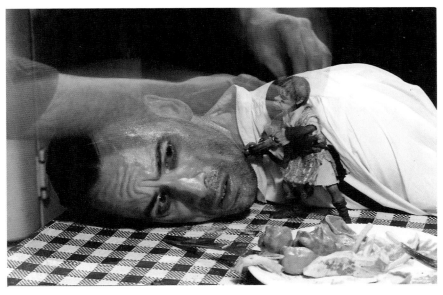

An animator from Bolex Brothers animates Frank Passingham during *The Secret Adventures of Tom Thumb*, 1986. (Courtesy of Dave Borthwick, Bolex Brothers, Bristol, UK.)

People, Objects, and Rigging
Organic and Nonorganic Objects
Shooting Safe Zones

People, Objects, and Rigging

Often with pixilation, whether you shoot the subject on a downshooter or horizontally, people and objects can be treated in the same way. This can be difficult on the person, especially when everything is treated like an object. It's almost inhumane to animate a human in pixilation for long periods of time with no support or break. As Nick Upton, the pixilated star in the 1986 Bolex Brothers film *The Secret Adventures of Tom Thumb*, states:

> Masochists *only* need apply. It's not for the feint-hearted or weak of spirit.
>
> In all but the wide (full-figure) shots, make sure there are "rock-solid" supports/guides/reference points, wherever possible, just beyond the edge of the frame, from which you can anchor and thus minimise any unwanted body movement. With regards to breathing, always capture the frame after breathing out, *not* in, as varying levels of stress, fatigue, or physical exertion can cause irregular intakes of air which can cause a "boiling" of the chest.
>
> **Nick Upton**

You will recall that when using actors in pixilation, it is important to try to get some sort of performance from them. This can be very challenging, as was the case for Nick Upton. Many of the successful pixilations from various artists tend to push the actors to exaggerate their emotions and expressions. It's also important to be able to hold expressions onscreen so the audience can see the emotion that is being expressed. I feel that you need to have a minimal of 20 frames to digest a particular expression. Usually more time is required and artists like Juan Pablo Zaramella actually use "freeze frames" to achieve this effect, since it is so difficult for a pixilated actor to hold a steady expression. Remember that we are constantly breathing, so that action will pulse our body in any expression or pose. I like to shoot my pixilated actor with several frames holding the same expression and then cycle those three or four frames over and over to get a consistent vibration while still eliciting the expression I want the audience to perceive. When directing a pixilation actor, it is best to start by making the large changes in the body frame to frame, and the last thing you adjust is the expression on the face because it is so difficult to hold an expression for too long. Try holding an expression like an extreme smile or a look of disgust for the better part of a half hour and you will see what I mean. If you can do it successfully then maybe *you* should be the actor in front of the camera. The face is often the last thing pixilated subjects account for, but ultimately those expressions can really sell an animated idea, because they pull us in with an empathetic point of view.

Adam Fisher, an independent animator from Maine, animated himself cutting his long beard and hair frame by frame as a metaphor for environmental devastation and overexploitation of natural resources in his 2010 film *Timber*. He needed assistance and support in the cutting of his hair while he placed himself correctly in front of the camera for registration. This took some careful planning and more careful execution. It took many, many months to grow his hair and

Figure 6.1

A sequence of frames from Adam Fisher's 2010 film *Timber.* (Courtesy of Adam Fisher © 2010.)

beard, and any mistakes in the cutting process could have been disastrous in the shooting process. This is his description of the process (Figure 6.1):

> To shoot *Timber*, I was seated in front of my computer with FrameThief open, and a camera pointed at me. Sarah assisted me. I would tell her when to take frames, and when to cut hair. I moved as needed, frame by frame, and would get into just the right position. Then I would say something like... "okay, trim everything above my finger!"
>
> We shot the sneeze first, with full beard. This gave us a chance to work out the timing. Once everything else was cut off, we simply repeated the animation without the beard. When I assembled all the frames, I just picked a good spot to switch from no beard to full beard!

Adam Fisher

Objects and people do need to be treated differently in order to get the best-animated results. In Oren Lavie's music video *Her Morning Elegance*, animated by Yuval and Merav Nathan, and in the British directorial group Shynola's *Strawberry Swing* for the band Coldplay, the human subjects were shot lying down on flat surfaces like a bed or a floor. Chris Martin of Coldplay was shot standing and lying down and was animated in various positions on the ground with a camera mounted in a stable position high above the ground plane. He still required support, but the supports could be hidden behind him, out of sight from the camera. In the 1986 ground-breaking *Sledgehammer* music video, Peter Gabriel was animated with lip movement. He sat upright and was given a head support to steady his head so the focus could be centered on his moving lips (Figure 6.2).

The main challenge in any stop-motion technique is how to fight gravity. With full-body support like a floor or bed the human figure can be animated freely in space with no constraints from gravity. This technique is similar to downshooting on a stand but in a grander scale. There are times when people or objects have to be animated with a visible support rig. This can be erased or cleaned out later in postproduction. We will get into more depth on this subject in Chapter 10. Any kind of prefabricated or custom rig can be used as long as it is strong, as small as possible, and relatively lightweight so it can be maneuvered easily (Figure 6.3).

People, Objects, and Rigging

Figure 6.2

Shot from Peter Gabriel's *Sledgehammer* with a support behind Gabriel's head. (Courtesy of Real World Music Ltd, Peter Gabriel Ltd, and Real World Productions Ltd.)

Figure 6.3

A series of rigs that can be used for a variety of situations.

Organic and Nonorganic Objects

I would consider humans to be a kind of organic object. Any object that has water as a base—humans, animals, plants, and anything that is alive—will be a challenge for the stop-motion animator. Over a period of time these organic objects will lose their water to evaporation and will change in form and color. Here is a very simple experiment that is worth the effort to punch this point home (Figure 6.4).

Figure 6.4

Three stages of water-based peas in a time-lapse sequence. (Courtesy of Marlee Coulter.)

Set up a DSLR camera, digital video camera, or webcam on a tripod and sandbag or tape it to the floor. Have the camera point down into a close-up of a pack of frozen peas (with the wrapper removed). Put a 650-watt light about 5–6 feet away from the peas and set the time-lapse interval for your camera at one frame every 10 seconds. This may take about 5–6 hours, but the change will be dramatic. You will see that the form and color change and that there is no stability in this kind of organic material.

Any object that is manufactured and devoid of fluids will be a more dependable and stable object to photograph, allowing you longer shoot times or intervals between frames. The conditions of the environment can really effect the composition of your subject matter. Plasticine (oil-based clay) can get warm under hot lights and start to shine. Certain organic materials like water-based paint can stiffen up if the environment is too cold. If you decide that you do want to shoot an organic object frame by frame, then the best approach is to work at a fast and even pace with no extended breaks so that the change in the object is small, even, and potentially imperceptible over the running time of the film. On the other hand, using organic materials will add another kind of movement and layer to your animation if that is what you seek.

The choice of objects that you use, whether they are organic or not, is critical to the overall effect of your animation. Objects can signify certain meaning and associations. PES, who has created many wonderful films, makes a point to carefully choose what objects he shoots. Here is his description of his intentional use of certain objects.

There's definitely a language of objects involved. I love playing with the layers of association that come with objects, and I strive to tap into these all the time. Examples abound in all my films. Take for instance, the boiling water in *Western Spaghetti*: I used bubble wrap to create this effect. It was uncanny how much bubble wrap could be made to look like boiling water. The effect was almost too good—too good because there are people who don't even notice it's bubble wrap until the 3rd or 4th viewing, and that means some people will miss the joke. Plus, bubble wrap has bubbles, just like boiling water. They have that very important detail in common, but you'd never imagine one could stand in for the other, no matter how much weed you smoked.

Another example in *Western Spaghetti* would be using the Rubik's cube as garlic. This gag is a totally different approach than bubble wrap because Rubik's cubes look absolutely nothing like garlic. I forged the connection by focusing on the act of ripping a clove of garlic from the head of garlic. In real life when you do this, you apply pressure with your thumb until crack! The clove comes loose. This action reminded me of when I was a kid and we used to take apart the Rubik's cubes and reassemble them into completed Rubik's cubes. This is something many kids remember from the 80s. You'd apply extreme pressure with a thumb to one of the corner pieces of the cube. It would be pressure, pressure, pressure, then crack!, the piece came off. Your thumb would kill, but it worked. It was then easy to reassemble all the pieces into a completed Rubik's cube. And, interestingly, that action is exactly how you get a garlic clove off. So, the humor lies in the unexpected connection, the logic I found there.

PES

Shooting Safe Zones

Subject matter is critical for a frame-by-frame film. Where you shoot plays an equally important role. As we have discovered, protecting and stabilizing your camera is very important in order to have control in the overall image. Light, shadows, environmental conditions, and power are all elements that have to be addressed in any stop-motion production. Naturally, if you shoot indoors or in a studio space you will have the option to control these elements. Natural light can be blocked out and simulated through staged lighting, if that is desired. Hopefully there are no erratic weather conditions in the studio, but there are a few issues that do need to be addressed in an indoor shooting environment.

The world is constantly changing. It breathes, expands, and contracts. Often this is too subtle for us to see, but time lapse and extended shoots over time will reveal this fact. Humidity affects interior spaces, and this can get to be a problem if a shoot goes over an extended period of time. Objects get heated and their molecular structure changes if kept under stage lighting for long periods, and if those lights are turned off for several hours or more then the cooling and humidifying process can begin. This will be influenced by what is going on outside the studio space. If you turn the lights back on and start shooting you will see a shift in the lighting and objects around the shoot when you compare the live frame to the previously captured frame. Trying to reduce the temperature and humidity fluctuations with dehumidifiers, air conditioners, and heaters can help stabilize shooting tables, tripods, cameras, flags for lights, reflectors, and objects that are under the camera. This is critical for more detailed and refined stop-motion techniques that require long shoots. Many pixilated films have such dramatic movement and changes in the overall image that they are more forgiving in this area. The changes in exposure and subtle movement of equipment in the scene often cannot be perceived. This reminds me of the practical approach that the Italian graffiti artist Blu uses when he shoots his painted walls around the world. He embraces the wildly fluctuating exposure and intentionally moves his camera frame to frame with slight adjustments so that erratic visual flutter-ing of the image becomes the norm. This allows Blu to stop and start shooting anytime he wants because he doesn't have to worry about an even and consistent exposure. This approach serves Blu's work very well because his painting process takes many days if not weeks to complete, and there is no way to maintain any consistency with all these wildly fluctuating environmental conditions (which include human traffic).

One other piece of equipment that many stop-motion filmmakers utilize is the voltage regulator. This helps keep the electrical input into a studio space even. The normal surges or spikes and drops in power can be avoided through these line conditioners and surge suppressors. Sola and Furman are leading brands in this equipment but there are several others. This could be an important addition to the stability of a controlled time-lapse event that is shot under controlled con-ditions in a studio. It's important to not have lights and exposure fluctuating so the natural change of an object in metamorphosis can be observed (Figure 6.5).

Shooting outdoors presents many unique conditions that must be addressed in order to make the most of the frame-by-frame approach. It's important to know

Figure 6.5

A Sola voltage regulator.

the effects of these elements so that you can attain the result that you seek. The single most important element, as mentioned previously, is the sun or lack of it. If you use the sun as your key light, then you must utilize the constant movement of light and shadow that will naturally occur. On a partly cloudy day, the sun will disappear and reappear, creating large fluctuations in your exposures. If you shoot over a long period of time, for example 2 hours or more, then the lighting will change dramatically from the beginning of the shot to the end. There is nothing wrong with these changes as long as you are aware of them. As we have stated, Blu is not concerned about the light changing because he wants the viewer's focus to be on the dominant drawn figure in the frame. He likes the peripheral movement and distractions, which help focus the eye on the subject. On the other hand, PES shot *Roof Sex* only on bright, sunny, blue-sky days in order to keep a consistent overall look to all of his exterior shots. In the 2007 Sony Bravia advert titled *Play-Doh*, animation director Darren Walsh directed his animators to move replacement, hopping, model rabbits at exactly every 90 seconds out in Foley Square in New York City. This way, the natural shadows cast by all of the tall buildings surrounding the square slowly and evenly moved across the frame in an intentional and nondistracting manner. Over 30 animators were equipped with walkie-talkies and given a signal to begin animating, with a constant second countdown so they knew when they had to complete their animation and get out of frame in order to keep that constant 90-second-interval shooting pace (Figure 6.6).

Another important issue that must be addressed is the stability of the camera. We have mentioned this before, but it is critical that no unwanted camera movements occur. When setting up a camera on a tripod, it is important to lock down all of the pan–tilt options that may be available on the tripod head. Tape down the legs to the floor if you are in a studio or use sandbags to weigh down the tripod if there is not an even, hard floor. Tripods with midleg spreaders offer more stability. It may be convenient to use small pan–tilt heads and lighter tripods, but if you are shooting outside, the wind and other elements like human traffic can threaten that critical stability. You may even consider a cable release for shooting your camera if you are not hooked up to a computer controller so you don't have to physically come in contact with your camera during a shoot (Figures 6.7a and b).

Figure 6.6

Evenly moving shadows on parked cars on Park Street, Bristol, UK.

6. Objects, People, and Places

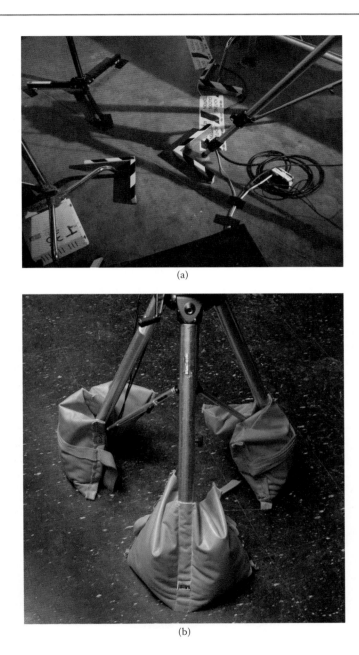

(a)

(b)

Figure 6.7

(a) A shot of taped tripod legs and (b) sandbags weighing down the tripod.

This kind of anchoring is necessary for motion-control systems, operated by hand or computer, and for all lights that need to remain in place so shadows and lights don't move in the scene. This is true for all frame-by-frame techniques, from pixilation to time lapse to shooting on a stand. It certainly is possible to shoot without this kind of lockdown approach, but the chances are that your lights or camera will be blown by the wind, bumped by you or someone on the set (since these are physically demanding techniques), or slip or move on their own over a period of time. After all, it is a wobbly breathing world and nothing is truly static. An accidental bump can be cause for a total reshoot. Although I advocate for a controlled and stable shooting space, it is important to note that some of these techniques are being used in a much more uncontrolled manner these days and that is the intention of the filmmakers. This adds a fresh look to the animation and certainly is very postmodern in approach. It is difficult to save a shot with an accidental camera bump in midshot. One approach to rectifying a bump to the camera is using a frame-grabber program that has an "onion skin" capability. If the camera has moved, then you can try to coax the camera carefully back into place. This may work if the action of your subject is active. It is much more difficult if the image has been static. Naturally, planning a cutaway and other filmic solutions can save a reshoot, but you have compromised your original intent because you didn't take the time to lock everything down (Figure 6.8).

The next area that we will cover all takes place in an interior or studio space. Downshooting, which still requires a camera, takes place on an animation stand that is housed in a studio with stage lighting. This area of frame-by-frame shooting has a wide range of approaches and materials. Let's examine some of these approaches.

Figure 6.8

A screen grab of two frames being ghosted or onion-skinned one on top of the other for placement registration.

6. Objects, People, and Places

PRO-File Keith Loutit

Keith Loutit. (Courtesy of Keith Loutit © 2015.)

Keith Loutit is an Australian filmmaker based in Singapore.

Loutit became an Internet and media sensation, following the release of his *Bathtub* series of short films, which transformed iconic and familiar Sydney scenes into miniature wonderlands.

Known as the pioneer of the tilt–shift/time-lapse technique, Loutit was the first to recognize how time and focus combine to support the powerful illusion of miniaturization in film. In his scaled-down and sped-up realities, real-world subjects become their miniature counterparts. Boats bob like toys in a bathtub, cars race like slot cars, and crowds march as toy armies. Loutit's aim is create a sense of wonder in our surroundings by "challenging people's perceptions of scale, and helping the viewer to distance themselves from places they know well."

Small Worlds is Loutit's most ambitious project to date, documenting the world's great cities, landscapes, and monuments of the ancient world in miniature. In a time of population explosion, impacts on our environment, and concern over limited resources, our world feels smaller than ever. But through Loutit's lens the world seems simple and uncomplicated, the differences between people are reduced, and obstacles seem easily overcome. By presenting a view of the world from "the outside in," Loutit aims to tell an inspirational story of mankind working together as one. We will see cities being built, the world's great events, and daily life all in Loutit's trademark style of miniaturization.

People and buses in Piccadilly Circus, London. (Courtesy of Keith Loutit.)

TDG: What do you want audiences to think after seeing your work? What is the impression you want to leave?

KL: The idea behind the technique is to perfect the illusion of miniaturization, and the goal is blur the line between what is real and artificial, in order to help viewers to see familiar places with fresh eyes, as if for the first time.

TDG: How do you determine the rate of time lapse with your subjects?

KL: Frame rates are as important to the illusion of miniaturization in film as the selective focus (macro blur). The idea is to make subjects move as their miniature counterparts would, such as toy boats, cars, trains, and animated characters. So the exposure time itself is fast to freeze the action. In terms of the capture/playback rate this is a recipe learned through trial and error that is applied differently to each subject, and is influenced by the scale of the scene as well as the speed and direction of subject action.

TDG: What kind of focal range do you use on your tilt–shift lens (18 mm, 24 mm, etc.)?

KL: When creating the effect in camera, I use modified enlarger lenses, and large-format bellows that allow me to tilt the lens more significantly than manufacturer brand tilt–shift lenses. To simulate changes in focus, or apply the effect on complicated subjects I create accurate depth maps, or z-buffers that allow for more precision. The focal length is not critical to the success of the illusion, although creating simple compositions that could plausibly resemble an animator's world is.

6. Objects, People, and Places

TDG: Do you use the intervalometer on your camera or do you use a separate time controller?

KL: I fire the camera using external intervalometers that are able to precisely fire the camera at what is often a very high rate of capture similar to a sports shooter's requirements, although for prolonged sequences.

Shot of Singapore's Gardens by the Bay. (Courtesy of Keith Loutit.)

TDG: What do you use to accomplish camera movement (motion control, etc.)?

KL: Due to the high frame rates, hyperlapse (shoot, move, shoot) techniques don't work so well as the prolonged time of capture spoils the ability to follow individual subjects. For this reason I prefer to lay long dolly tracks that create a reasonable perspective shift on wide landscapes.

TDG: Have you used other forms of time lapse?

KL: Yes. My current project documents the changes in Singapore's skyline from over 50 camera positions, recording 3 years of construction and demolition activity to date. Once completed I hope it will be the first time an audience will see an entire city growing in great detail, without the typical visual artefacts present in long-term time-lapse photography.

TDG: Do you use a lot of postproduction work on your stop-motion production or do you like to do all the effects and clean up "in camera"?

KL: There is a lot more postproduction involved in high-quality tilt–shift work than is apparent at first glance. I often blend various elements such as clouds, traffic, and people that are all shot at different capture rates. I also perform detailed scene modelling and depth mapping to perform animated focus effects and push different light/times of day through a scene.

TDG: How do you market your work? What is the intended audience?

KL: I have never promoted my work beyond releasing it in a short film format on YouTube and Vimeo. The works are personal and artistic in nature, usually appealing to an audience who is already familiar with the scenes before the technique has been applied.

Shot of people in Trafalgar Square, London. (Courtesy of Keith Loutit.)

TDG: Do you have any advice for artists, animators, or novice filmmakers that want to try your methods of using frame-by-frame shooting?

KL: Most of the technical challenges and decisions about using tilt–shift lenses vs. postproduction can be researched and solved easily enough. In my opinion the work in the style that really stands out as being exceptional are the films where it is obvious that the director understands historical styles of stop-motion animation and uses subject selection, light direction, and landscape composition to create simple charming animations. I would also advise anyone attempting this style to shoot during twilight or sunny days using soft sidelight to simulate an animator's lighting setup. Other time-lapse styles unrelated to the technique often destroy the illusion in the viewer's mind. An example would be to avoid long traffic light trails at night, which detracts from the stop-motion feel of the style.

7

The Multiplane Downshooter

Two shots of Joan Gratz Studios, one from earlier film days and the other showing her newer digital setup. Photograph by Joan Gratz. (Courtesy of Joan Gratz © 2010.)

A Stand of Your Own
Lighting for the Downshooter
Clay, Sand, and Dimensional Objects
Cutouts
Backgrounds

A Stand of Your Own

There are several elements that define the multiplane downshooter. The most distinguishing factor is that this type of shooting requires an animation stand. Immediately you might think that this can be a very expensive proposition. You would be right if you decided to use a more traditional animation stand, like an Oxberry stand. This is a fairly complex piece of machinery that has the capability to have compound table moves underneath a camera that can crane up and down. The movement is usually controlled by a computer and requires stepping motors that move the various parts in small increments. This was the preferred method of shooting traditional cell or drawn animation (Figure 7.1).

Most independent downshooting artists make custom stands that can be as simple as a mounted piece of glass that is placed in front of a camera on a tripod. Many artists cannibalize old stands and cobble together parts depending on their needs. It is not necessary to have a moving table or camera, especially these days with postproduction options. So analyzing your needs and building something that is appropriate and affordable is a manageable proposition. When I shot the *Penny Cartoon* for *Pee-wee's Playhouse* in the early nineties I put together a stand out of two-by-four boards of wood with a glass shooting surface and a mount for a camera. It worked beautifully and serviced my needs quite readily. The camera was locked in position with the lens pointing downward onto a stationary glass surface.

Figure 7.1

A traditional Oxberry animation stand. (Courtesy of Oxberry LLC, Carlstad, NJ.)

All the motion was created by animating the models and materials across the glass. Neither the camera nor the table needed to move.

The tabletop that holds the objects, cutouts, or various materials to be animated can be a hard flat surface of wood or heavy solid plastic, but the great majority of shooting surfaces on downshooters are made of glass. This allows for light to be transmitted from underneath, which can be used for mattes and other silhouetting techniques like sand animation. The glass also allows for objects on the glass surface to be shot without any shadows falling directly below those objects. This is important for cutout animation and green-screen matting. We'll get into these approaches a little later in this chapter. The glass itself can be any ordinary glass, but there are a few advantages to choosing the right kind of glass. It is important to note that glass is preferable to Plexiglas because the plastic is less stable under the heat of the lights and scratches more easily. The best glass to use is called "water white glass." It has no tinting in it, transmits 98% of the light, and usually has an antiglare and antireflective coating. This allows the backdrop to be photographed so that the true colors of the artwork show through. This can be an expensive choice and is not absolutely necessary because of the ease of color correction in post. All glass will slightly change the look of the background artwork. You just want to minimize that influence. It can also be helpful to have a dark ceiling, dark cloth, or board or wall opposite the glass so there is a minimum of reflection that goes back onto the glass (Figure 7.2).

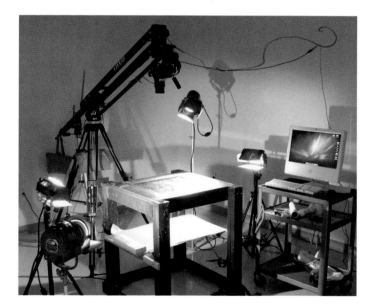

Figure 7.2

A custom animation stand used for shooting the *Penny Cartoon* with a piece of water white glass.

Lighting for the Downshooter

The downshooter does present some very specific challenges when it comes to lighting. Shadows are the issue. When an object or cutout is placed on the glass shooting surface, it will cast a shadow through the glass down on the lower plane, depending on the height of the lights and the distance between the shooting planes. This isn't necessarily a problem unless you are trying to shoot on green screen or if you don't want large and graphically confusing shadows being cast from one plane to the other (Figure 7.3).

There are many parameters to determining the distance between the shooting planes:

- How wide can the bottom plane be, based on the shooting range of a 35-mm or longer lens?
- How high above the shooting plane does the key light have to be for a good effect?

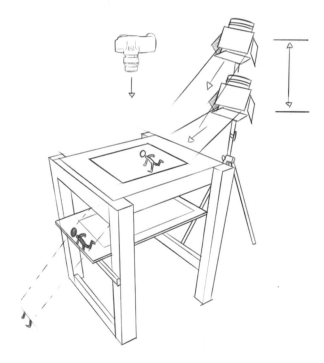

Figure 7.3

Key light position relative to the shooting table and the shadows caused by objects on the top plane.

7. The Multiplane Downshooter

- Do you want to shoot horizontally or will you shoot at a 15- to 45-degree angle by tilting the table?
- What kind of depth of field do you need to achieve?
- The size of the object you're animating and the distance it needs to move.

The two-by-four stand I built has about 16 inches between planes and the camera was mounted about 2 feet directly above the first shooting plane. As a result, my key light, no matter which side it was on, could rise from 1 to about 20 inches above that plane before objects on the top glass plane would cast visible shadows onto objects on the lower plane. You should think of lighting dimensional objects on a stand in a similar fashion to lighting those objects in three-dimensional space. The key or primary light needs to define the object clearly, set a mood, and bring out the three-dimensional form of that object. Your key light can be placed anywhere, 360 degrees around the shooting table. It can be placed below the glass, shooting up through the glass, or anywhere from the glass shooting surface up to the point where the object shadow falls on the lower plane and can be visible to the camera. Ultimately, you must be aware of reflection of the light on the glass and the possibility of lens flare (Figure 7.4).

Key lights can create deep shadows, so it is often smart to give some definition to the shadow areas on dimensional objects with some fill light. This goes back to the three-point lighting topic we covered earlier. The range of the fill light is similar to the key light for the same reason: shadows. The fill will usually be

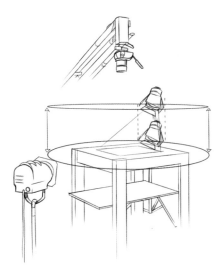

Figure 7.4

The range of the key light on an object on the top shooting plane that doesn't cause shadows on the lower shooting plane.

Figure 7.5

The range and placement of the fill light on a downshooter with dimensional objects.

placed on the opposite side of the key so it can complement the stronger key light and slightly fill the shadow area. This fill should be diffused and not wash out the shadows that the key light creates. Both of these lights can utilize colored gels to add more atmosphere. Oftentimes directors of photography think about light from nature. In this case, the key light would be warm (yellows and reds) like the sun and the fill light would be cool or in the blue range, which is normally found in the shadow areas and reflects the ambient blue light from the sky (Figure 7.5).

Shooting cutouts, which are usually flat graphic images, traditionally have a much more restricted range for lights. The lighting has more to do with allowing the artwork to be read clearly and with even lighting. Traditional drawn animation is shot on a stand with two key sources of light set at the sides of the stand at 45-degree angles to the shooting surface. The lights are set equally above the shooting surface so that there is an even flat lighting effect. Bryan Papciak, a successful DP and director, describes his approach to lighting these surfaces:

> Focus each light into a hard "spotlight" aimed across the table to the opposite side. The light on the left side of the table would be spot-focused to the right side of the artwork, and the light on the right side of the table would be spot-focused on the left side. Once the two spots are balanced, then defocus both lights to "floodlight." This will result in the most even coverage across the table.
>
> **Bryan Papciak**

Because cutouts are flat paper or similar material, they don't cast shadows on themselves. On a traditional animation stand the artwork is placed under a hinged piece of glass that rests on top of the artwork once it is placed on the table. This glass is called a "platen." The glass platen is more difficult to contend with in cutout animation because it will constantly move or displace the artwork if the artwork sits loosely on the glass shooting plane. Tacking down or sticking the cutout artwork to the shooting surface with wax, Blu-Tack, or tape will help eliminate this problem.

The last area in lighting we need to examine is the "underlit" or bottom light setup. This technique is used to gain a silhouetted effect of the objects that sit on the top glass shooting plane. There is usually no light from above in this approach, and so the objects or cutouts block the lighting that comes from underneath the artwork, creating the silhouette. There are a couple of ways that the light can shine from the lower plane to achieve this effect. A light box that has florescent tubes and a diffused white milk glass surface can be mounted on the lower plane to radiate an even, bright light. The other approach is reflective in nature. Similar to the evenly lighted top surface approach, two lights can be mounted on either side of the stand, focused down at 45 degrees on the lower plane. There should be a sheet of white or colored card that the light hits, reflecting up directly under the top glass shooting plane (Figure 7.6).

Carolyn Leaf, a master and pioneer in downshooting techniques, describes her own setup:

> I have given many sand workshops and the set up is a single framing camera over a piece of clear glass (plastic builds up static electricity which can make the sand jump around) with white paper underneath, raised and underlit. I like to put 2 lights on either side of the glass pointing down onto white paper and bouncing back up to the glass surface. This gives even lighting and isn't too hard on the eyes, which shouldn't look directly into lights and can find tiring the contrast of light and dark when working with underlit sand.

Carolyn Leaf

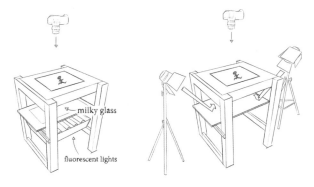

Figure 7.6

Two underlit setups for downshooters.

Clay, Sand, and Dimensional Objects

"Downshooting" refers only to the shooting setup, but the objects or material that can be animated are quite varied. This is limited only to the imagination of the animator or designer. There are several mediums that have been used successfully, and we'll touch on a few. My own experience with downshooting primarily focused on clay figurative subject matter. This is when characters are drawn and then sculpted in Plasticine (an oil-based clay that never hardens) in relief. This approach to clay animation has a stylized graphic quality that looks like a mixture between two- and three-dimensional animation. The great advantage to this technique is that no armatures or support structures are required to hold up the puppets. They lie on the glass and can be moved around anywhere in space without the constant struggle with gravity that is a part of most dimensional stop motion. It is necessary to fabricate replacement models if the figures need to turn in three-dimensional space (Figure 7.7).

Academy Award–winner Joan Gratz works with clay and oil on glass. She paints the Plasticine with tools and her hands on the glass, and the images carry great detail and texture, constantly metamorphosing from one image to the next (Figure 7.8):

> One of the virtues of painting with plasticine clay is that it has tangible dimension and unlimited textures. It has that hand made quality because it is. Because I am painting and making changes to the same canvas the images seamlessly flow into each other.
>
> **Joan Gratz**

Sand is a very flexible medium to animate on glass. This can be lighted from the bottom or top or both, depending on the effect desired. Many animators

Figure 7.7

A relief Plasticine sculpture shot on a downshooter by Wonky Films. (Courtesy of Wonky Films, Bristol, UK, © 2010.)

Figure 7.8

Images from the Academy Award–winning "clay painting" film, *Mona Lisa Descending a Staircase*. (Courtesy of Joan Gratz © 1992.)

use sand to block out bottom lighting. The sand is brushed and stroked with tools or by hand on the glass surface. The thinner the layer of sand, the more light can penetrate the sand, giving edges a feathered look. The more dense the sand, the more opaque and black the image appears. Carolyn Leaf describes her approach to sand animation:

> It is very important to me to show the texture of the material I am working with. For sand animation, the lighting is adjusted so that a suggestion of the pile of sand within and forming the silhouette of the drawn figure is visible. I want the audience to know sand, but sandiness doesn't dominate the storytelling. Likewise with wet paint, I make sure that my finger-pushing movements show so that everyone knows that it's paint.
>
> **Carolyn Leaf**

It's important to use darker sand if you are trying to achieve the silhouette effect. Some white sands will pick up the slightest bit of light, which can reveal the effect. On the other hand, you may want to see some of the sand and show its texture as Carolyn Leaf suggests. It's important to test these effects out before committing to an approach. The shooting surface needs to be more horizontal when shooting sand because it sits unattached to the glass and can easily drift down the table because of our old friend, gravity. Plasticine has a bit more adhesion to the glass and the shooting surface can be slightly tilted up to a 35-degree angle. The great advantage of this is that it is easier on the animator's body. Craning over a horizontal table all day long in order to see and manipulate the artwork can be much more demanding than sitting and seeing artwork that is tilted up for better viewing and access.

Shooting objects under a downshooter has its own challenges. The objects that can be used are limitless. I have seen coffee beans, candy, Barbie dolls, hair, coconut shells, pencils, and so forth. The only restriction is the size of the object and whether the object needs to have additional support beyond the surface of the glass. These various objects have more flexibility with lighting, as mentioned earlier. It is important to light for the dimension and form of these objects. The higher off the glass the object is, the more possibility there is of a reflection falling from that object back onto the glass. One solution is to polarize the lights and the camera lens. These filters and gels can be found at any decent photography or film store. Polarized filters reduce reflections but don't always totally eliminate the problem. Polarizing lights and lenses also increase the contrast of the image, which is not always desirable. The background plane also plays a role in how much attention you pay to reflections and smudges on the glass. When you shoot a green-screen backdrop, the dirt and reflections are less of an issue because you will eventually eliminate them in the keying process. The only potential problem with these smudges and fingerprints can come when they intersect the contour of the object to be keyed. We will discuss the role of backgrounds shortly.

Cutouts

The largest technique in downshooting is "cutouts." This area could warrant a book on its own because of its deep history and varied applications. The cutouts can be original illustrated artwork, photographic in nature, figurative or abstract. It's a fairly direct and inexpensive technique, so early on in filmmaking designers, directors, and animators explored this form. We mentioned Lotte Reiniger, whose *The Adventures of Prince Achmed* was the first cutout feature animated film ever made in 1926. There have been countless other cutout animated films from every country in the world that supported animation because of the direct and inexpensive approach. This includes the 1983 film *Twice upon a Time* by American director John Korty and Charles Swenson.

Most cutouts are animated on a traditional animation stand or a custom downshooting stand, but there are some other approaches that we will discuss. A majority of cutout films tend to be on the figurative side with a certain narrative involved. This is because images can be drawn or cut out of magazines and pieced together in a collage technique. Reiniger used cutouts with a backlit approach, creating very detailed silhouettes. But more contemporary artists like Terry Gilliam from *Monty Python's Flying Circus* and Evan Spiridellis, one of the founders of the successful Internet entertainment company JibJab, use top-lighted original artwork and photographic images. Figurative images are cut apart appendage by appendage (legs, arms, heads, etc.) and then reassembled under the camera with the ability to be manipulated frame by frame. Finally, Yuri Norshtein's *Hedgehog in the Fog* is an example of an elaborate and beautifully executed use of this technique (Figure 7.9).

Animating these small pieces of card, plastic, or paper can be delicate work under the camera. There are so many free-floating parts that can be bumped or accidentally moved. Various techniques are practiced to gain a little control over this form of animation. The two issues are stabilization of cutouts on the shooting (glass) surface and the movement of appendages like arms, legs, and so on and their consistent relationship to each other. The first issue of cutout stability on the glass shooting surface can be addressed by the weight of the paper, plastic, or card being used. The heavier the weight of the drawn or clipped image, the more it will stay put on the glass. Tacking down this heavier paper with tape or wax can make a huge difference. Lotte Reiniger used thin lead sheets with her silhouette cutouts. I am not suggesting this approach, but thinner paper can be

Figure 7.9

Cutout body parts from 2009 Year in Review from JibJab. (Courtesy of JibJab, Venice, CA, © 2009.)

mounted on Bristol card or lightweight board which will help the image from being so easily brushed aside. Artists even use double-stick tape or small pieces of sticky wax under the cutout. The glass releases the adhesion of the tape or wax quite easily, but there may be a residue that remains on the glass. The animator has to be vigilant to these cutout footprints by cleaning them up during the shooting process when necessary. There is a tacky material called "Blu-Tack" that many cutout artists use because it leaves less residue.

The second challenge with cutouts, especially cutouts that are figurative in nature, is the consistent relationship of one cutout to the next. For example, if you create a cutout character that walks, the legs have to pivot or be jointed from the same point on the hip for each movement or frame. Hinging these elements together is the solution for this kind of relationship. There are many different approaches to hinging cutouts. The most effective approach is to purchase a hand rivet set. The rivets will be slightly visible and thus must be integrated into the design of the animation. Another approach that is a bit less intrusive is to use small holes in the cutouts and then wire them together with very thin wire strung between the holes. The last technique I will mention is the use of sticky microcrystalline wax between the cutouts. This last technique requires a little more scrutiny on the animator's part because the pivot point can drift over several moves, but this technique is quick and less visually intrusive. Blu-Tack can be used in place of the wax. Many times cutout artists only tack down larger cutout sections of the body like the torso and leave the arms untacked so they can be easily moved. The head and arms usually move a fair amount more than the

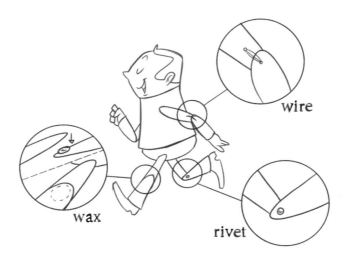

Figure 7.10

Three methods of cutout hinging (rivet, wire, and wax).

torso, so this approach makes the animation go faster, although it does require a delicate touch. This last tack-down technique of hinging has the added benefit of allowing the animator to incorporate the classic "squash and stretch" animation technique to the character. Because the cutout puppet does not have fixed positions for the hinging, the animator can compress and stretch the placement of the various parts, giving a little more dynamism to the animation (Figure 7.10).

There are many more techniques for gaining control and hinging cutouts. It all depends on your ability to work under the animation stand, how patient you are, and what your style of work and animation is. As Evan Spiridellis puts it:

> For cut paper animation we don't use any hinges. It's a bit more frustrating and time consuming to work this way but it allows a lot more flexibility in the poses and keeps the animators from tightening up. If we are working with paper-puppets we'll use anything we can twist into a circle as a hinge. Sometimes it's wire, sometimes it's a paperclip. It's typically whatever is lying closest on the desk.
>
> **Evan Spiridellis**

Two final pieces of advice from director and animator Terry Gilliam regarding cutouts:

> The most important equipment was a sharp scalpel.
> Make sure you blacken the edges [of the cutouts].
>
> **Terry Gilliam**

Objects and cutouts can also be shot vertically as opposed to in a downshooting mode. Pictures can be mounted on glass or mounted sliders that hold the cardboard-backed cutouts upright. The camera would be mounted on a tripod in this case. The lighting arrangement is a little more flexible and tracking the cutouts becomes very manageable. Jim Blashfield, a contemporary independent artist and American Animation Master from Portland, Oregon, would often shoot objects vertically frame by frame and then cut out those photo images and reshoot the photographed images on a downshooter. Here he describes his approach to a music video he directed called *And She Was* for Dave Byrne and the Talking Heads in 1986. It was produced by Melissa Marsland.

All scenes were animated to the frame by frame log we had made of the song. That log was the backbone to the video, whether scenes were preplanned or improvised. Also central were the boxes of color Xeroxes that resulted from our guerrilla-photo-shoots all over Portland. We drove around looking for garage sales, second hand stores, interesting neighbourhoody things, and photographing them on site, along with personal items that seemed to fit in: A mailbox that looked just the right way, etc. For one overhead scene Don (Merkt) sent Melissa (Marsland) off to snatch a couple of pairs of my underwear from our house, the patterns of which appeared floating across the scene. We chose ordinary things that either we thought would be amusing, or/and which seemed to have embedded metaphorical power, or which we otherwise thought should be honored for their long and unappreciated contribution to our lives. Spatula, reclining chair, purse, party hat—icons from the less appreciated heights of our culture. We also carefully photographed our pixilated moving leg sequences, and others, one frame at a time, onto color slides, and these were cut out by a herd of our friends with X-acto knives, and put into the boxes in folders. The live action of David singing was 16mm footage which we shot in Dallas in our very minimal live action shoot—camera balanced on some videotape boxes in David's office in the back of an old house they were renting—which we then turned into paper prints at the Portland State library microfiche department. We rented two 35mm Mitchell animation cameras which we mounted on homemade animation stands made from 4×4 lumber, plastic gutters, threaded rods, conveniently sized 8×10 glass plucked from picture frames from a local store and hinged with duct tape, etc.

Looking around for someone who shared our aesthetic to go off and shoot slide sequences of the other band members who were scattered around elsewhere, we found that our friend (like us, usually underemployed) Gus Van Sant was willing to hop on a plane and returned a few days later with more slides for the Xerox machine. Many others, most of whom went on to work in our next videos, participated in the making of this video.

We had 28 days from the day we got the go ahead until it appeared on MTV. We had no idea of the huge impact it would have (Figure 7.11).

There was no significant post production in *And She Was*—maybe an hour to clean up something or other. It was all shot under the camera, images stacked up in layers, one frame at a time. All the lateral "pan" effects were done either on threaded rod with runners attached or on repurposed slide rules as I had done with *Suspicious Circumstance*.

Jim Blashfield

Figure 7.11

Images from behind the scenes of *And She Was*, a music video for David Byrne directed by Jim Blashfield. (Courtesy of Jim Blashfield and Associates, Inc., Portland, OR, © 1985.)

One other independent director and animator from the Boston area, Daniel Sousa, also works in this vertical multiplane frame-by-frame technique. His 1998 film *Minotaur* is an example of this approach. Here's how Dan describes his process (Figure 7.12):

> Most of the character animation was originally hand-drawn on a light table, cut out and mounted on rigid cardboard. This was done so that each replacement could stand up vertically within a three-dimensional set. The set was then lit with fiber-optic lights and shot in stop motion, using a 16 mm Bolex camera. Some of the animation was done as hinged cut-out puppets on glass, using a multi-plane rig.
>
> **Daniel Sousa**

Backgrounds

The final subject that I need to cover is the background or bottom shooting planes on a downshooter. There have been downshooters and traditional animation stands with many more than two shooting planes. The same issue of shadows being cast on one plane from the object on the shooting plane above it still exists. That means that multiplane downshooters need to be pretty tall

Figure 7.12

A still from Daniel Sousa's 1998 film *Minotaur*. (Courtesy of Daniel Sousa © 1998.)

and are often cumbersome to operate. Depth of field becomes an issue with multiple planes. The many levels of glass also diminish the light levels on the lower planes. As a result, the lights need to be brighter so a deep depth of field can be achieved on a lens like an *f*/22. Longer shutter speeds can also be utilized to allow more light and smaller iris openings. Most stands use two planes with dimensional objects being stacked on top of each other on the top shooting plane. Many times, dimensional objects like candy, coffee beans, or a sculpture are shot on top of a green screen or chroma background that allows the object to be pulled off that background in postproduction. That object may be composited onto another image later with proper planning. The downshooter is ideal for green-screen work for the following reasons:

- The image on the top plane usually gets very little green spill light from the layer below. (This is the light that reflects back up onto the model from below and tints the edges of that model, making it hard to pull a clean chroma matte in postproduction.)
- There are no shadows on the lower level from the object. (This is because your lights have been set to prevent top plane object shadows from falling on the lower plane background.)
- The lower level is lighted evenly, which is perfect for pulling the matte in postproduction. (Even chroma-key–green background layers are easier to matte out in postproduction.)

Figure 7.13

A shot of Joanna Priestley working on her downshooter for the 1986 film *Candyjam*. (Courtesy of Priestley Motion Pictures, Portland, OR, © 2011.)

Practical backgrounds on the lower shooting plane of color, illustration, light, or any other form are equally effective with the downshooter. When I shot the *Inside-Out Boy* for Nickelodeon and the *Penny Cartoon* for the CBS television series *Pee-wee's Playhouse*, the figures were made out of Plasticine on the top plane but the backgrounds on the lower plane were either cutout paper or pastel drawings. The lighting can be altered below to create any kind of atmosphere, but cutouts and slightly elevated objects or paper on the background will have immediate shadows that are cast directly down on that plane under the artwork. Cutout artwork on the background layer should be glued down to avoid shadows. The shadows will distract from the crisp, graphic, refined edges of the artwork and diminish the quality of the overall picture, so they must be addressed. If you want to have animated backgrounds, then consider drawing them or shooting the background animation on a second sheet of glass with a color on a level below that. Joanna Priestley, another successful independent artist and animator from Portland, Oregon, describes her setup (Figure 7.13).

> I shot *Surface Dive* on my homemade, multi-plane animation stand to add depth to the compositions. I had the replacement sculptures on the top level, a huge variety of clear glass pieces on the middle level and large, animated pastel drawings on the bottom level.
>
> **Joanna Priestley**

PES, whose work we saw in previous chapters, shot a very complex downshooting project for Honda called *Paper*. He utilized paper photos and illustrations along with the hands of the creators and animators in the shots. It's a wonderful piece of animation and this is how he described the project (Figure 7.14):

> With Honda, I tried to make this spot much more than a typical downshooter. The idea of 2 minutes of straight downshooter sounded boring to me, especially

Figure 7.14

Shot of the PES Honda shoot, looking down on the downshooter "on steroids." (Courtesy of PES © Honda 2015.)

when dealing with the twists and turns of Honda's 70 years of automotive design, which are by nature varied and complex. There are so many vehicles, so many inventions ... it called for something more exciting, more complex. So, I sought a shooting approach that mirrored that "long and winding road" quality of their design history, something constantly changing and shifting.

I found my answer in the idea of unhinging the camera and allowing it to examine that idea board from different, constantly changing angles, not just from directly above. This blew the whole thing open and transformed the film into a totally new beast. The camera moving off axis meant that the illustrations would also have to respond to those constantly changing camera angles, and would allow me to experiment with optical illusion drawings in a way I had not seen anyone do in animation before.

Of course, the flip side of that was it ushered in countless production challenges, but fortunately we had the money and talent to solve them. So, to answer your question, *yes*, it's a downshooter, but it's on steroids.

PES

There are many practitioners of these art forms working across the globe. Independent filmmakers often still utilize these techniques because they are affordable, conceptually appropriate to their style, and these techniques stand out in today's contemporary computer-driven industry. Programs like After Effects, TVPaint, and Toon Boom have been mastered to elicit a very refined cutout style with more control and efficiency. The "photo puppetry," drawn 2D computer, and composite approaches of these programs have dominated this form of animation

---

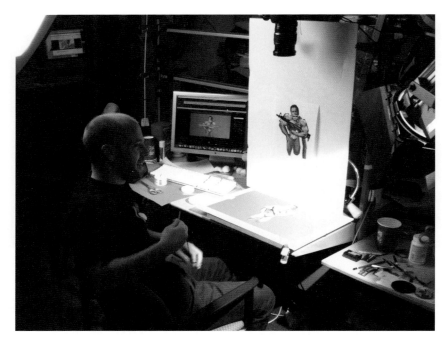

Figure 7.15

A shot of an animator Kevin Elam at JibJab on their custom downshooter. (Courtesy of JibJab Media, Inc., Venice, CA, © 2010.)

for over 15 years in the commercial world, but there are still many "holdouts" who like to dabble in the old school approach to cutouts, like Evan Spiridellis and his team at JibJab (Figure 7.15).

As you can see, there are many different ways to build or cobble together a downshooter stand, and many artists put together their own version of this piece of equipment. Many years ago when I was working for Art Clokey, the creator of Gumby, my partner and I took on a job in the evenings. The "clay-on-glass" technique was required and I had to put together a stand to produce this night-owl production. The drawing below is the final stand that I put together. It is very rudimentary in construction but it is solid and still operating 26 years later. It was inexpensive to build because I used two-by-four pine lumber, carriage bolts 5 inch long with a 5/8 inch diameter, two 30 × 24 inch ¼ plywood sheets and a piece of glass. The bolts allow you to take this stand apart so it can be moved or adjusted. At the time I was shooting with a 16-mm Bolex camera, but these days the camera mount holds a Canon DSLR with a zoom lens. I built a second downshooter stand to produce a film called *Ain't No Fish*. I had less space to work in so I built a tilted stand that was mounted on commercial workbenches that had adjustable vice-grip tops.

Figure 7.16

A second, smaller downshooter stand with tenting.

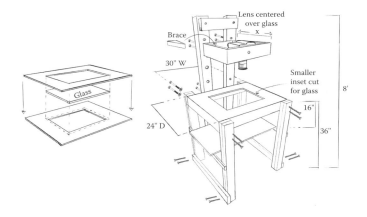

Figure 7.17

A diagram of a rudimentary 2 × 4 inch downshooter stand.

I tented the stand with black fabric so there was reduced reflection from the environment. There are better designs for a downshooter stand, and there are adjustments that can be made to these stands to improve them (like mounting a simple track on the back column that would hold a camera and allow for tracking zooms), but these simple stands will suit most of your needs in the downshooting realm. Good luck with your downshooting. It can be a lot of fun! (Figures 7.16 and 7.17).

8

A Sense of Drama

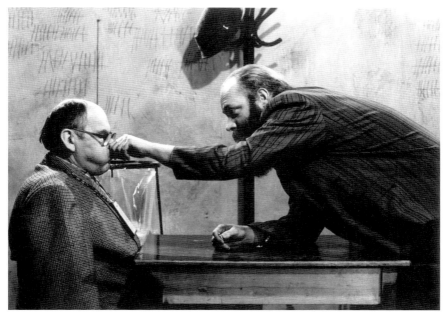

Image from *Food*. (Courtesy of Jaromir Kallista and Jan Svankmajer. © 1992. Athanor Ltd, Film Production Company, Jaromir Kallista and Jan Svankmajer.)

Live Action and Single Framing
Subtle and Broad Performance
Reference Film and the Cartoon
Look in the Eyes

Live Action and Single Framing

We have already mentioned how important it is to exaggerate images and actions with some of these alternative stop-motion techniques. Time lapse usually does not include acting or contrived scenarios, but it still requires a sense of drama if you want to capture an audience's attention. Choosing the right subject matter that will reveal real transformation over time makes this technique effective. Setting the camera so that the composition is dynamic becomes important to a time-lapse study or any form of filmmaking. This can be done by utilizing foreground and background elements in the same shot, thinking about the use of diagonal lines in the composition to lead the viewer deeper into the composition, placing the camera in an unusual point of view, playing with scale and by including an interesting color and lighting palette. An artist also has to consider how a composition will change over the course of a shot. Knowing where your camera will move and what will transform in front of the camera is critical to maintaining great dynamic compositions. It's usually more interesting to have a subject enter the camera composition from a diagonal direction and not directly in from the side. There are many ways to build interest in your animation and many of these principles apply equally to live-action filmmaking (Figures 8.1 and 8.2).

Figure 8.1

A series of shots showing dynamic composition elements (foreground/background, diagonal lines, unusual point of view, and color palette).

8. A Sense of Drama

Figure 8.2

Using scale for dramatic effect in *Alice* by Jan Svankmajer (1988). (Courtesy of Jan Svankmajer. Photo © Athanor Ltd Film Production Company, Jaromir Kallista and Jan Svankmajer.)

Good art direction is critical to any film, but there are two more elements that are even more important. The first element and the one that everything rotates around is the idea. We touched on this in preproduction, and Focal Press has several titles that cover this immense subject. The next element is performance. Having good actors can make or break any film, and the same is true with animation. When it comes to animation, you (the animator) are really the actor and what you do with your inanimate object, person, or artwork in terms of performance is pivotal to the success of your film. Live-action filmmakers know that there are two kinds of realities. First, there is the way life unfolds from one event to the next. We live this reality every day here on Earth. Sometimes it's exciting and usually it is not. Life is full of dull tasks and activities that are necessary to our survival. When we go to see a film or a stage production, we do not want to be reminded of these mundane tasks and realities. We are interested in the compressed, interpreted high and low points and emotional expressions of an event. We want the icing without the cake. This is true for animation as much as any other sequential art form. One example of this reality in animation is the use of the everyday walk. Walks can be very revealing about an individual. When we observe a walk we take cues about the energy level, determination, and attitude of an individual. If this is essential to understanding that character, then animating a walk is an important element in the storytelling. But normally we don't really need to see a character walk from Point A to Point B. We want the filmmaker just to get us to Point B and move the story along. We are interested in the emotion and highlights of the story and not the everyday realities, like a long walk. There are some exceptions to this premise, but for the most part this is the dramatic reality that animation should consider.

PES describes his approach to his 2003 pixilated film *Roof Sex*. Even though he approached this film in documentary form, there is still a great sense of drama and compressed and interpreted shot sequences.

> Would the idea of 2 chairs having sex conceptually work as a drawn animation? Yes, definitely. In CGI? Yes, definitely. But, in my opinion, the execution gains power when using real objects on a real location … it's much, much closer to real life and it hits a more absurdist note. I believed that stop motion was the best technique for *Roof Sex* because my intention was to treat the idea like a documentary. I fancied myself spying on these two specific chairs that escaped from their owner's apartment one day and, almost as a voyeur, I recorded what they had done for posterity. There are no cartoony sound effects; everything was done with an eye to being as believable as possible. As in much of my work, there is humor to be found in the earnest—almost documentarian—approach to the fantastic. For me, photographic images combined with absurdist, yet oddly logical, ideas are like rubbing two rocks together to create a spark.

PES

Subtle and Broad Performance

Time lapse usually does not include performance except by the natural occurrence of an event. So this single-frame technique is not included in this subchapter. There can be some subtlety in performance in some of the downshooting techniques like sand animation. This more refined movement can be achieved with small controlled moves in the sand or clay and can even be attained by the use of dissolves from one frame to the next. Yet on the whole these alternative frame-by-frame techniques are broader and less refined than other forms of animation, like drawn and computer-generated animation. There is more control in these latter techniques and they are often used in this way.

Generally, like action on the stage and in early film, broad acting is assigned to the wide shot. The figures or objects are smaller in the frame (like seeing the stage from the back of the theater), so the action has to be bold and broad. Close-ups are usually reserved for the more subtle and refined movements of an individual or object. In pixilation, these more subtle forms of acting are more difficult to achieve because of the constant movement of a human, which is caught frame by frame. The constant moving in and out of registration or exact placement of the person in the frame makes this technique broader and less subtle. Broad, exaggerated expressions help distract the viewer from the constant vibration even in close-ups. Although I do not often use freeze frames because they stop the lively and active frame, potentially pulling the audience out of the film, they can be a solution for reading emotions and expression clearly. You can also repeat two or three similar frames in edit to keep the vibration going, although if this is done for too long the viewer can see the cycle of frames. Extreme control on the subject or actor's part is one very effective way to achieve some sort of subtlety in pixilation. It recalls Lindsay Berkebile's expression "chaotic life amongst silence." Controlled breathing and eye movements along with rig support for heads and hands help maintain stability and potential subtlety without breaking the special energy that is prevalent in pixilation.

There is the potential for more subtlety in object animation and downshooting because the objects are inanimate and don't live and breathe (at least not until they are projected). The subtle or broad approach, style, and purpose is up to the director. Examining the work of PES again reveals a lot of wonderful and controlled movement, like in the underwater world of *The Deep*. Chains are moved with gentle, S-curve gestures that mimic a piece of kelp waving underwater, and calibers bob up and down like jellyfish as plier-fish surge forward, all underwater (or so it appears). These beautifully animated tools create that illusion because of the subtle yet dynamic choices the animators make in the movement (Figure 8.3).

Joan Gratz produces beautiful, full detail paintings and uses metamorphosis to move from one to the next frame by frame. These can be dissolved from one image to the next or they can be step printed. Step printing means that each frame has a low opacity layer of the previous and following frame on it. Step printing is also referred to as "step weaving." This adds to the flow and subtlety in her animation. As Joan puts it:

> In *Mona Lisa Descending a Staircase* images of the human face are subtly transformed to communicate the graphic style and emotional content of key artworks of the 20th century.

Joan Gratz

Figure 8.3

Image from *The Deep*, PES. (Courtesy of PES 2010.)

We have covered broad facial exaggerations that many artists like McLaren and Kounen utilize, but it is important to remember that dynamic movement also makes a huge difference in the performance. Certainly by using "eases" you build in acceleration and deceleration, but there is much more to movement than this single dynamic principle. This is the essence of animation. There is so much to discover in this area that even veteran animators like myself are constantly trying new combinations of movement for dramatic effect. Here's an exercise that I often use in the many workshops I have conducted around the world. I usually demonstrate this in three parts, but the most important two parts are illustrated below. It is natural, as demonstrated by many attempted pixilation films seen online, to break down movement in evenly paced or measured increments. This elicits a rather robotic result. So I like to move a subject across the frame evenly to see what that looks like. I then introduce "eases" and then "dynamics" in motion. Try this exercise and see how fun movement can be, especially when you add a few principles of animation to it (Figures 8.4 and 8.5).

You will need a digital camera (still or video camera) and a tripod. If you have a laptop to control the camera, then bring that along, but this exercise can be done without the capture software. You will need a flash card in your digital still camera to capture frames that you will download into a computer after the exercise if you don't have a computer on set. You will also need a person, but an object will work. You can shoot this exercise outdoors or indoors, but

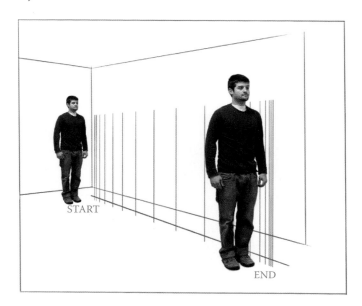

Figure 8.4

A shot of movement that includes ease-ins and ease-outs.

8. A Sense of Drama

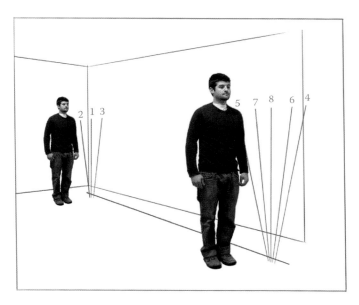

Figure 8.5

A shot of the "dynamic snap" animation setup.

you will need about 20 feet of space to move in. Try to find a background with very little visual detail, like a wall. If you are outdoors, then try to execute this exercise where the light is as even as possible. If you are indoors, you will need broad soft light, like overhead lights. Set the camera up slightly off-center from your subject, who will stand 20 feet away from the camera (frame left) near the wall. Mark off 15 forward positions for your subject to move toward the camera, ending frame right. Try to include some simple ease-ins and -outs. Remember that these are the increasing and decreasing increment movements that are a natural part of the physics of any movement. Shoot 15 still frames of your subject in the far position, then have him or her move up to the next forward mark (toward the camera) and shoot two frames at 30fps. Continue this pattern until the subject rests near the camera (including those ease-outs), and then shoot 15 frames of hold at the end. That's the first reference.

Try this again, but this time hold for 15 frames at the front, lean your subject back a bit in anticipation (shoot two frames), then one small move forward (this position is optional); shoot two frames, then move your subject all the way up to the last position (close to the camera), leaning forward (two frames), then one frame leaning back, one frame leaning forward (not as far as the first time), and so on. Settle your character out and shoot eight frames of hold. The playback should be 30 FPS. This is the "snap" effect and makes your subject look like a vertical diving board. It's very dramatic and adds a fun dynamic to your shot.

Reference Film and the Cartoon

One of my first jobs was working for the Claymation studios of Will Vinton. A small crew of us spent many years animating characters for a Claymation feature. Many of us were relatively new to animation, so one of the techniques that Vinton incorporated was making a live-action reference film of all the voice actors as they read their lines in the sound studio. Each animator would take the appropriate clip of live-action reference film into their set and view it on a 16-mm viewer as we animated. It was a great way to learn how movement works and there were actions that the voice actors incorporated in their performance under the direction of Vinton that we were able to translate into stop-motion animation. This gave the director more unified control over the performance of the animation. The more successful animators only used this reference as a bouncing board for animating and incorporating more dramatic expressions, holds, and actions in their puppets. We used this same technique using digital video cameras more recently when I animated on Aardman Animations *Creature Comforts America*.

The important point to make is that even the most experienced animators can rely on reference footage. It's a wonderful learning tool but one that is to be interpreted. Many times I have students and workshop participants make reference films and then manipulate that footage in an editing program like Premiere. Frames from the reference film can be repeated, footage can be slowed down or sped up, frames can be "rock and rolled" (meaning the edit goes backwards and forwards several times on a chosen group of frames), and there are many more manipulations that can be done on regular live-action reference film through the edit process. This is like testing, but in the edit, not under the camera. The reference film is not for public consumption, but just to see how things work in real time and to give the filmmaker ideas about how to adjust the frame-by-frame shooting to achieve certain effects and push certain emotions. When working in front of the camera, animation is best when it does something that live-action cannot do. Pixilation has the look of live-action when you view the individual frames, but it is the relationship of those frames, one to the next, that makes this art form interesting. When you start playing with the incrementation and variation of the placement of the human subject in the frame, then you enter into the realm of the moving cartoon. This approach is exemplified in the pixilation work of McLaren, Kounen, Jittlov, and PES and can be realized by trying out the exercise just mentioned.

Another habit that I highly encourage and will mention again is "testing." It is our nature to be conservative with animation movement, but if you allow yourself the opportunity to experiment with movement and frames without the pressure of making a "finished" shot, then you may discover certain effects and movement that are unnatural but highly effective and entertaining. See what you can get away with in your movement tests. Oftentimes certain movements that are illogical and unexpected can give you just the right feel or effect, but often it is testing that can lead you to that conclusion.

One technique that many pixilation filmmakers promote is the use of the wide-angle lens. This can add to a cartoon, dramatic effect that can be humorous. These lenses range from 12 to 35 mm in focal length and usually are best when they are prime, or single focal length, lenses. The wider lenses are most effective but are also expensive to purchase. Using an 18-mm lens on human faces can be very dramatic, humorous, and even bordering on the grotesque. When you use a wide lens like a 24, 28, or 35 mm focal length on animated objects, it helps bring you down into that object's world and scale. Using a wide-angle lens for close-ups when the lens is set at "eye level" to the object helps make the image appear larger than it actually is, because the lens makes the background recede faster than a longer lens. The foreground subject looks larger than the background, giving it a grand appearance. This close proximity of the lens and camera to the object can make it difficult for an animator to get to the animated objects, but the effect can be worth it. The only area where wide-angle lenses can be a problem is in the downshooting mode. Wider lenses require wider background shooting planes, and this can be impractical. Most downshooting stands are made for 35 mm and longer lenses—35, 50, 85, 105 mm and so on. Any dramatic quality such as distortion has to be incorporated into the artwork. As mentioned previously, longer lens like 85, 105, and 135 mm have an inherently shallower depth of field than wider lenses, so it's important to consider this if you have artwork on a down-shooter background that needs to be in focus. Oftentimes a lens in the 35–50 mm range works well on downshooters as a general rule.

Look in the Eyes

Audiences have to care about your characters. Whether your performance is broad or subtle, stylized or naturalistic, photographic in nature or fabricated from nuts and bolts (literally), they have to have a humanity to them. It's critical that the audience have an empathy and vested interest in what your character will do next. If you don't explore these emotional avenues then you will lose your audience. Allowing your characters to appear to think, have an emotional response, and then react with action gives them a kind of life that we understand. So much of that thinking and emotion can be read in the eyes. It is critical to bring the camera close in and allow enough time for your character to think. This makes them real in the eyes of the audience. The close-up is certainly the animator's friend. These shots can have a huge impact on the story and require the least amount of work. A few blinks, the darting of the eyes, or a slight squint can carry a scene with great emotional power. We do understand the attitude of a personality from their body language. Are they energetic, depressed, or nervous? We can read this immediately because the body is large and consistent in its form, but it is the eyes that confirm the true emotional state. Since we can't hear the character think, we then become more involved in the film by starting to project our thoughts on them based on the situation and our understanding of the character. We may be right or wrong. It doesn't matter. What is important is that we participate in

Happiness

Sadness

Anger

Surprise

Fear

Disgust

Figure 8.6

A series of images of eyes displaying the six universal emotional expressions.

the storytelling through our projections and caring, and that's good filmmaking. This focus on the eyes explains why early film actors and stage actors would wear heavy eye makeup to highlight their eye expressions. The audience in the auditoriums needed to see what their eyes were saying. Two other sources to study regarding the use of eyes are Chuck Jones' book *Chuck Amuck*, where Jones writes about eyes and timing being at the heart of a thinking animated performance. The other source is a wonderful 1928 silent film by Danish-born Carl Dryer, called the *The Passion of Joan of Arc*, where the whole emotional storyline is expressed through the actors' eyes.

Paul Ekman, a prominent psychologist, showed and proved that there are several universal emotional displays across all cultures. These include happiness, sadness, anger, surprise, fear, and disgust. Audiences all understand these expressions and displays of emotion immediately because we all share them, and they are revealed through the eyes as much as by any other means. These expressions and emotions should be used and exaggerated in frame-by-frame animation for a greater dramatic effect (Figure 8.6).

9

Rhythm and Flow

Image from JibJab (Walter Cronkite, Farrah Fawcett, and Ed McMahon). (Courtesy of Evan Spiridellis.)

Let the Music Lead
Patterns of Movement
The Beat Goes On

We really like to base our animation on music. Usually what we do is, first Merav edits the drawn animatic over the sound track, creating a general tempo for the whole piece.

Then while doing the 3D animatic we fit the more subtle movements and gestures to the bits.

Yuval Nathan

Let the Music Lead

When I first started studying film I had a wonderful teacher by the name of Martin Rennalls. His love and passion for filmmaking were immeasurable and his high regard for music and sound left an impression on me. He would say, "Mr. Gasek, the sound that you create for your film should have as much weight as the picture itself. Sound must be half of the film and no less." I had never given this much thought until Martin brought this to my attention. As I started to analyze the films that I followed, I realized that this statement rang true. I am a very visual person, like many filmmakers, and since I am creating visuals for my film the sound would often fall into the shadow of the pictures. One day I decided to give a live musical performance for one of the film exercises I was screening for Martin's class. I brought in and played a guiro, which is a hollow, ribbed cylinder of wood that is played by rubbing a stick across the ribs. This sound, along with the rigging of the sailing ships that I filmed, made an unusual combination that somehow worked and garnered high praise from Martin. From that point on I promised that my sound tracks would play prominent roles in all of my films and I have never regretted that commitment.

Ever since the early days of animation, music has played a key role. Some animators have followed music and sound effects to the frame and others have let the sound track become more interpretive and less connected directly to the images. Both approaches have strengths and different effects on the audience. When the music is synchronized directly to the picture, then the music drives the picture. If the sound track is interpretative, then the visuals tend to lead the meaning and effect of the film. This is also reflected in the way these two approaches are produced. With synchronized music, the music is created first and broken down in length to the frame. The animator takes those sounds and accounts for them on a log sheet or "dope sheet" so every single frame has an associated sound. This is also the way lip-sync dialog is created, as we saw in an earlier chapter. The pictures or mouth shapes follow what the sound dictates. In an interpretive approach to music, a composer or sound designer is given the moving image, even if it's not completely finished, and starts to create a track based on the general movement and mood of the pictures. Sound effects are usually created this way but require very specific placement on the timeline so they are synced up to a specific image. Occasionally original sound effects can be created first and the picture actions follow the broken-down analysis of that sound on a log sheet.

William Kentridge, the South African artist and animator, describes his approach to sound tracks:

> Work with the composer starts after about the first two weeks of filming. We look at the rushes, listen to different kinds of music played alongside the images. From here the film and music go back and forth between the composer's studio and mine, in an ever-tightening observation.

William Kentridge

The great majority of films are produced in this fashion and there is a lot of interpretation, spontaneity, and creative flow with this production protocol. It is important to work with a composer or sound designer who has experience with moving image sound tracks and who understands the rhythm and flow of a narrative or experimental production. Working with a pre-existing sound track and following that track to the frame is a lot more work, but the results can be very potent. Here's an exercise that will give you a taste of this exacting marriage of sound and picture (Figure 9.1).

This exercise starts with a music track. I recommend creating an original music track from a program like GarageBand. You certainly can use a composer or make a music track in any other fashion that is easy and effective. The key to this music track is that it needs to be simple, short (5–15 seconds long), rhythmic, and only featuring one or two instruments (preferably with no lyrics). Get that music track into digital form, like an AIFF file or a WAV file. Investing in a program like QuickTime Pro can make a big difference in

Figure 9.1

A waveform from sound in Dragonframe.

creating picture and sound tracks. It is also important to note that you need to record the sound track at a rate that you will use for animating, so the picture and sound don't lose synchronization. If you are shooting at 30 FPS then you must record at that rate. If you choose to stick to a film rate of 24 FPS, then record at 24 FPS. Import that sound track into a program like Dragonframe, Premiere, or even Final Cut that allows you to import sound tracks, shows a waveform for the sound, and has the ability to count every frame and its associated sound in the whole timeline. Our website will list several programs that are good for sound breakdown. Dragonframe does this quite readily and provides you a log sheet, waveform, and associated area for potential visuals.

Create a log sheet (illustrated earlier in this chapter). Start stepping through the music track with the forward arrow key frame by frame and locate each sound and the beat or rhythm of your composition. I find wearing headphones really enhances this activity. It is necessary to scrub through or play the music in running time as well as just breaking it down frame by frame so you get an understanding of the inflection and dynamic of the musical composition. Write down the sounds and their placement by their associated frame number on the log sheet. The waveform will help you see the dynamics in the music and the regular patterns like the beat. Some sound-reading programs like Magpie Pro and Dragonframe print out a waveform right on their existing log sheet format. This is convenient but not necessary. Once you have your whole music track broken down into frames and recorded on your log sheet then you are ready to animate.

You can use any one of the alternative photographic stop-motion techniques that we have been reviewing, but one of the easiest approaches is to work on a flat surface with objects. Similar to other exercises, you will need a digital video or still camera, a tripod, a few small lights, and a solid and stable tabletop. If you use a program like Dragonframe, then you need to import or load your sound file into the audio timeline. The nice thing about using Dragonframe is that you will have your sound file on the desktop with a total frame count and waveform. The sound will automatically sync up with your picture frame and you can proceed to animate to your sound track.

Try to choose objects that are related thematically or visually to the style of the music you are using. For example, if your music has a Japanese flavor, you might consider animating chopsticks and Ningyo dolls; if your music leans toward hip-hop, you might animate sneakers and baseball caps; if your music is light and floating, you might animate feathers and paper. I think you get the idea. Keep in mind the things that you are interested in animating and allow that to influence your choice of music when you create the track. The objects can be pulled in and out of frame, manipulated and moved based on the beat, sound, and exact frame count of the music. You can move and place your objects around the frame in a way that is similar to the look of the waveform, with lots of activity when the waveform is large and less movement when it is small. I find it is helpful to assign a particular object to a particular sound or instrument for clarity. Have fun with this exercise. It will take more time to animate this way because of the constant reference to the sound track. I'm sure you will be pleased with the results.

Patterns of Movement

One can consider frames of animation like musical notes on a scale. This is especially true when visuals are closely linked to the sound track. Generally, when a waveform rises in size on the audio track, the corresponding visual frame will be active or more detailed, reflecting more energy and dynamism. If the sound recedes, then the corresponding image may remain static with little dynamic change. One master of this approach to visual music was Norman McLaren in his many film experiments, including his 1959 *Short and Suite* and the 1971 *Synchromy*. McLaren used many different techniques, including drawing directly on 35-mm film with pen and ink. He also used optical printing techniques in *Synchromy* to create a direct visual link to the sound track (Figure 9.2).

Similar to music, when an animated sequence is highly active it can be exhilarating to watch. Too much exhilaration can be exhausting and the audience can start to drift away. It's critical to let your frame and characters rest, even for just a moment, so the audience can catch up, digest what is happening, and maybe even get a sense of character and thinking from an animated subject. This is practical and adds dynamic range to any composition.

Even with the lack of a sound track, object movement and visual frames can have patterns that create certain effects and illusions to the eye. These patterns become recognizable to us because we know their movement despite the fact that the objects are not necessarily related to that movement in real life. We saw this in the work of PES. His candy-corn flames and his pepper heart are great examples of movement that have a distinctive pattern. *The Pepper Heart* features three or four red peppers in increasing size that are replaced one after the other. The first and smallest pepper is held for about eight frames, then

Figure 9.2

An active sound track and the corresponding visual timeline.

Figure 9.3

A series of peppers simulating a heart. (Courtesy of PES.)

each pepper is replaced with a larger pepper. There is a brief hold (four to six frames) on the largest pepper, then the peppers are replaced with smaller peppers (the same three or four peppers), then the smallest pepper is held for eight frames, and so forth. PES uses a loop or cycle of movement mimicking the repetitive beating of a human heart. This creates a visual music of sorts that can be appealing to the eye. The hold along with the changing pepper movement make this a successful sketch (Figure 9.3).

William Kentridge follows his own intuitive approach to movement and patterns. In his *7 Fragments for George Melies*, which is part of an exhibit that has traveled around the world in major venues, Kentridge gives his artwork a life of its own through the use of stop-motion drawing and reverse playback techniques. The artwork of one of his drawings appears to sink to the bottom of the frame until Kentridge enters the picture, frame by frame, and rescues the slumping image. When I asked Mr. Kentridge about his approach, here is how he responded:

> The morning I decide to make a film, I begin. I may have to pause to find an object or image. Thinking about the film starts while setting up the camera … I can make a film without having to sell the idea to a producer. I can practice my craft without being dependent on the whims of anyone else—there is no crew, no cast. I like to use a camera like a typewriter.
>
> In the long term, my approach is based on a year at the Ecole Jacques Lecoq in Paris, where there is an emphasis on the expressiveness of gesture throughout the body. In the short term, I find the trajectory of a movement either by watching myself in the mirror, or filming myself or other people with a video camera; or by making a movement in the air with my hand, while counting.
>
> Objects and images in the films float between being seen as photographic objects, or the things themselves, and provoking other meanings and associations—for example a cloth draped around a corkscrew is also a woman lifting her arm.
>
> **William Kentridge**

His animated movement is lyrical and so is the pattern and pace of his animation. It unfolds in a mysterious yet simple pattern that makes us wonder about the life of the created image (Figures 9.4 and 9.5).

9. Rhythm and Flow

Figure 9.4

William Kentridge rescuing the image in his artwork in "Moveable Assets," from *7 Fragments for Georges Melies.* (Courtesy of Marian Goodman Gallery, New York and Johannesburg.)

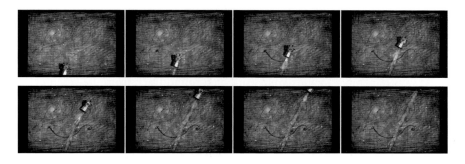

Figure 9.5

A series of images from "Voyage to the Moon," *7 Fragments for George Melies*, William Kentridge. (Courtesy of Marian Goodman Gallery, New York and Johannesburg.)

This rhythm and flow of images can be an abstract concept to grasp, but it is often the element that defines a particular piece of animation. It is the artistry. Whether the visuals are tightly matched to a music track or much more interpretive in nature, there does need to be a driving force to carry the film along. Once again we turn to the clay painter Joan Gratz:

> I am interested in creating a "visual onomatopoeia" in which line, color, movement and rhythm create the feeling of a particular experience without illustrating it.
>
> **Joan Gratz**

The Beat Goes On

Often these alternative stop-motion techniques can be employed in the marketplace in the world of the music video. Part of the reason that this formula works is because these photographic stop-motion techniques can be produced on lower budgets and in shorter time periods. Ultimately it requires a great idea, a good piece of music, and sweat equity. These techniques, especially pixilation, can require a lot of hard physical work, as we have discovered. More importantly, this technique allows audiences to see artists in the magical world of animation with a certain rhythm of movement that cannot be recreated in live-action. The Peter Gabriel music video *Sledgehammer* was an early example of this approach, and there have been numerous examples of similar uses of pixilation over the last three decades. The one approach that makes pixilation more time-consuming is if the filmmaker decides the human subject has to lip-sync or mouth the words of the song. This requires more detailed preparation and production, and it can be difficult to get exacting results. The subtleties and in-between movement of the human mouth are something we recognize instantly, since we watch each other speak every day. When it is not done exactly the same way, especially with the photographic image of a human subject, then it doesn't sit quite right. This stylization of animated speaking can be humorous but difficult to pull off, because the mouth shapes are not exacting and it is difficult to get human subjects to emote believable expressions that would normally be associated with words.

Always remember to start your work on a sound track from the very beginning of your animated film preproduction. It is totally up to the filmmaker on how they want to use a sound or music track, interpretative or literally, but it is always important to infuse that sound track with great importance so that it carries half of the weight of your film. The image itself has its own rhythm and flow on a timeline, and once sound is introduced there should be a kind of synchronous dance between the two.

I'll leave this chapter with the words of Julian Tryba, the "layer-lapse" artist, who relies on music to elevate his visual time-lapse work.

> Music is at least half of the final product. I wish I didn't rely so heavily on music because it can be hit or miss and it's crucial. I know exactly what kind of sound I'm looking for and I follow a lot of artists so I get exposed to a lot of music. Finding an amazing song is like trying to find a partner, there are plenty of options but most of them are not a good fit.

> **Julian Tryba**

PRO-File Corrie Francis Parks

Corrie Francis Parks animates sand, paint, and other unusual materials. Produced with one hand under the camera and the other on the computer keyboard, her work maintains an organic connection to natural materials and traditional production methods while fully integrating digital technology.

Shot of Corrie Parks working in her studio. (Courtesy of Corrie F. Parks © 2013.)

Her award-winning animated shorts have screened at Annecy, Hiroshima, Ottawa, and Zagreb and at major festivals on every continent except Antarctica. She looks forward to the day when she can count penguins among her biggest fans.

TDG: How long have you been working in stop-motion animation?

CFP: I started out in hand-drawn 2D animation and spent many years honing that technique. I began doing stop motion in graduate school in 2002, when I made my first sand animation film, *Tracks.* After that, I jumped back and forth between the two doing depending on the project so I guess it's been about 13 years now.

TDG: How much preproduction do you do before shooting in this technique? Please briefly describe your preproduction approach.

CFP: I will usually thumbnail out sequences in my sketchbook and often I'll do some test animation before committing to a big scene. This comes from back when I used to shoot on film and there was no second-guessing.

Everything had to be perfect for the shoot and you wouldn't know until the film came back from the lab. Now I use Dragonframe so I have a bit more security. Sometimes for a particularly complex shot I will animate a rough guide by hand ahead of time and use that as a line-up layer. But I also like to leave room for improvisation so I don't want to have everything too planned out. Sometimes the sand will want to go a certain way and it's good to have the flexibility to follow where it leads.

TDG: What kind of equipment do you use (i.e., camera, software, lights, post-production software)?

CFP: I use a Nikon D810 with a variety of prime lenses that allow different angles. I light the sand from below on a 24 × 36 inch lightbox my husband made from faux wood flooring panels, under-cabinet lights, and a large piece of tempered glass. I capture frames with Dragonframe and use Adobe Lightroom to process the frames, and Photoshop and After Effects to tint and composite the footage afterwards.

Shot of a close-up of sand on the stand. (Courtesy of Corrie F. Parks.)

TDG: What is it about your approach to stop-motion animation that most appeals to you? Please describe why sand appeals to you and if you consider your work downshooting.

CFP: I definitely consider this downshooting—the camera is pointing down when I shoot! What I like about sand is that it is both two-dimensional and three-dimensional. The sand is a physical material that can be piled and moved as a mass, but it becomes a flat silhouette on the screen. I also love the purity of light hitting the camera lens and sensor. When I animate with sand I am animating light!

TDG: Did you build your own stand? How did you customize it?

CFP: I've gone through several camera and lightbox setups. My camera is mounted on a very tall tripod with a boom arm that allows me to raise and lower it depending on how close I want to be to the shooting surface. I do all of my camera moves in post so I never move the camera during a shot. I built my own lightbox because I wanted a bigger surface to work on and there really weren't commercial lightboxes that were affordable for me. Now that LED technology is so prevalent and affordable, I think I might switch to an ultra-thin light table. I'll let you know how that goes!

Shot of Corrie Parks' animation stand in her studio. (Courtesy of Corrie F. Parks.)

TDG: How closely do you work with a sound track? Please describe your picture/sound relationship.

CFP: I think very carefully about sound from the very beginning stages of a film, but usually hand off the film to a professional to do the actual music and design. In *A Tangled Tale*, I wanted the sound environment to reflect the unique aspect of the film—the organic and digital methods of production intertwining. My sound designer, Cole Pierce, recorded sounds of water and ambience tracks and mixed them with sounds created electronically. There were dozens of layers in the effects so that the sound retained the mysterious quality.

TDG: How important is the movement or animation in your film work?

CFP: Coming from a character animation background, having smooth, fluid movement is very important to me.

TDG: Do you think the type of stop motion that you use lends itself to humorous subject matters or can there be a serious approach achieved? What makes this technique humorous or serious?

CFP: I think sand definitely tends more towards serious and moody animation because of the gradients of darkness and light that come naturally from the material. It's like working with a liquid Rembrandt painting, and can be atmospheric. But I think it also has the potential for humorous moments because it is a silhouette medium and is similar to shadow puppet animation. So it really depends on the artist's sensibility.

TDG: Can you achieve a performance from an object or person using your stop-motion technique? Is it important to have an emotional trigger in your work?

CFP: I definitely look for a performance from the sand. It has its own personality and in fact different sands from different places have different personality. A very fine sand will cling to itself and leave dusty residue on the glass as it moves along, creating a particular kind of trail. More granular sand will catch the light and sparkle like prisms and it will roll around in independent grains, not sticking to one particular spot. Some sand builds up static and clings to fingers or brushes or jumps around the glass in weird ways. So you have to get to know the personality of the sand you work with, optimizing its strengths and making allowances for its weaknesses.

As far as an emotional trigger goes, that is more of a narrative choice than a material question. In all my films I want to take my viewers on a journey through the film. That might be through a traditional story arc or through a more abstract visual experience. But in either case, the viewer should come out the other side of a film having changed in some way.

TDG: Please give a short description of how you use After Effects and the multi-layering process.

CFP: I shoot the sand with a DSLR so I have a sequence of animation as my raw footage. If I am planning to layer elements in a scene, I will shoot each layer of animation as well as background layers separately. Then I take all of these various layers into After Effects and use several different compositing techniques to get them together. Compositing sand is tricky because the fine grainy texture around the edge of the sand catches the light and creates a halo that is difficult to remove with keying. The method I use depends greatly on the type of footage I have and the end result I am aiming for. The simplest approach is to apply a Multiply blending mode onto the sand animation so the white will disappear and the black will multiply onto the layer below. This works in some situations, but I also will use the paint bucket effect, animate masks around certain areas, and sometimes even create a track matte by hand to get the best blending of the layers. My After Effects files usually have hundreds of layers!

A shot from *A Tangled Tale*. (Courtesy of Corrie F. Parks.)

TDG: How do you market your work? Who is the intended audience?

CFP: I try to make films that everyone can enjoy, but that ask to be watched more than once. I like to make my audience work a bit to understand a film and also leave the door open for multiple interpretations. Everyone brings their own experience and history to every film they watch and I want my viewers to connect with the film in their own context. I love going to festivals and hearing what audiences think the film means. I always get different answers.

TDG: Do you have any advice for artists, animators, or novice filmmakers that want to try your methods of using stop motion?

CFP: Have fun with the materials! A lot of artists start out trying to do something very detailed and precise and the experience can be frustrating because sand or wet paint are hard to control and messy. I recommend starting with abstract movement and morphing shapes because the fluidity of the material and the process of animating straight ahead lead into that naturally. Once you are more familiar with the specific materials you have under the camera, you can start to impose more limitations on them. But the process should always be enjoyable, or else why bother?

TDG: Are there any other points that you would like to make regarding your stop-motion work, past or present? What areas do you want to explore in the future?

CFP: I am interested in exploring the digital hybrid methods associated with sand and paint on glass further. I think the potential has barely been tapped. That was a big motivation for writing my book *Fluid Frames*, which goes into these techniques in detail. I hope that with more animators exploring these material-based methods, we'll start to see some real innovations in the technology.

10

Collage (The Digital Advantage)

A series of composites of a fish on various backgrounds wearing various hats by Tom Gasek.

Planning a Collage
Match Lighting and Rotoscoping
Clean, Clean, Clean
The Chroma Key

Planning a Collage

Even in the early days of filmmaking, the idea of combining images was compelling and artists like George Melies were fast to practice this approach. Mattes were often used to block out certain areas of the exposed film frame and then the camera reexposed the film (after it was rewound to the beginning of the first shot) to a new image in the blackened area. Working with film made the process of combining images in collage much more difficult than the present-day digital approach. In film, effects had to be combined directly in the camera or in an optical printer, which was developed in the 1920s and 1930s. Optical printers are rarely used anymore, but they became quite sophisticated in the later part of the 1980s, just as the dawn of digital compositing came into play. They involve one or more projectors that focus exposed, developed film directly into a film camera with great precision and control (Figure 10.1).

Since the great majority of moving images are created digitally these days, compositing various images and frames together is much more accessible. A good computer and software like Photoshop, After Effects, Shake, Blender, and Nuke make this possible. These programs are not cheap, but they are more affordable to use than optical printers or even high-end professional post-house programs.

Figure 10.1

An optical printer. (Courtesy of Academy Award–winning optical printer artist Eugene Mamut.)

Many of these programs offer free 30-day trials and wonderful discounts for educational purposes. We'll get into some of these techniques, but first we need to explore how to prepare for a composite or collage project.

Why would you choose to composite images? There are certain aesthetic decisions that an artist can make that determine whether he or she composites images. This is not something that can be easily pinned down. The combinations of imagery that can be paired together open up a huge area of visual imagination, and many artists are curious to open that door. Quite honestly any combination of figures and images can be combined together to serve any idea. There are also many practical reasons to composite images. A filmmaker may not be able to find two images that can be placed together, like an elephant and the Empire State Building or paper hearts that might surround the heads of lovers. In cutout animation, this juxtaposition of unlikely images can easily be achieved under the camera in one pass. We saw this in the work of JibJab, Terry Gilliam, and Jim Blashfield. Photographs and drawings can be cut out with a scalpel or scissors and prepared for shooting under the camera. Anything is possible with this approach. Ultimately, as mentioned previously, new cutout animation has become the ultimate digital composite form. This new cutout animation, which utilizes programs like Flash, Toon Boom, and After Effects, composites images electronically with layers and lots of fine control. In any cutout, pixilation, time lapse, or other animated compositing, the consistent lighting of images is critical for a unified composition. Shooting images with similar camera lenses also builds consistency. The other important aspect that needs to be considered is how these images are going to interact. If they are figures, will they have to look at each other? Will their eyelines match up? Will the objects or figures cross over each other? Do you want to have shadows fall from one object to the other? These and other questions need to be addressed as you prepare for your composite work.

Match Lighting and Rotoscoping

There are several ways that you can start to combine images in a test to make sure that they work together to your satisfaction. But before we explore that, let's talk about lighting. When you have different objects or people that you want to put together in one frame or image, you need to decide on a unified lighting plan. Your key object or person should be lit to match the atmosphere that you want to have in the final collage or composite. This might be the classic three-point lighting we discussed, or it could be a high-noon sun from an outside shot or even single-source lighting in a studio. Once you have established that lighting, then all of the other objects that you shoot that will be combined with your main image must be lit with the same lighting scheme. This includes any gelling or filtering of lights. This can take a lot of planning and careful coordination. If you can't control all the lighting with the various objects, then you will have a final composite image that looks pieced together and not natural (Figures 10.2 and 10.3).

Figure 10.2

A matched-lighting composite image.

Figure 10.3

A composite image where the lighting of the objects doesn't match.

10. Collage (The Digital Advantage)

An adequate solution to uncontrollable lighting is to light all objects with flat overall lighting. This will unify the objects when they are placed together, but flat lighting is dull and does not highlight the dimensional quality of your objects or people. Keep in mind that you can improve these images in color and contrast in a composite program like After Effects. One hint for helping to match images is to shoot your objects in a low-contrast lighting situation where there is enough fill light in the dark areas. This way you will have the important detail from the image that you can color and contrast correct after you have the whole composite image put together (Figure 10.4).

The other important element to consider when combining images is the placement and eyeline of those images or figures. Once you place the various images together in one frame, you want to know if they will have a relationship to each other based on their visual connection and image dialog. If you had two people who were being animated separately and you had to put them together, would it feel like they were addressing each other? One way to gauge this relationship is to take the most difficult element or person to animate of the composite and then animate it. You can then import this movie into the rotoscope function of a program like Dragonframe. When you animate the second element or person for the composite, the rotoscope function will allow you to onionskin or ghost each frame from the initial footage to each frame of your new animation. You can see where your new object or person needs to be adjusted so it has a relationship with the initial image or person for every frame you animate. This will make your final composite much more controllable. One element that can help sell the composite technique is the shadow of the composited image. It is often difficult to take the

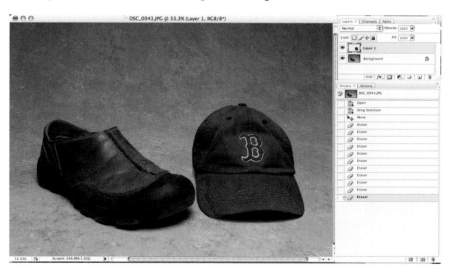

Figure 10.4

Objects that have been blended together with flat lighting.

shadow of an image, cut it out, and blend it in with a new image. This is because the shadow is not solid and when it is cut out it brings with it the image of the area that it is shading, which may not blend into your new composite. One solution that many composite artists use is to create your own new shadow for the cutout composite image in After Effects or Photoshop. The trick they use is to copy the layer element (of your composite image), flip it, and place it below the original object or element. Turn the copy black and lower the opacity to 20% or 30%. Then you need to transform it and angle it so it looks like it's on the ground or wherever it needs to fall naturally in the new composition.

You can also take one image into Photoshop and then open the second image. You will have to do a rough cutout of the key element in the second image with

Figure 10.5

An onionskin rotoscope image.

Figure 10.6

An onionskin comparison in Dragonframe for eyeline.

10. Collage (The Digital Advantage)

the lasso tool and then drag that element onto the first image. This will give you a quick and general idea about how the images might match in lighting and position. (Figures 10.5 and 10.6).

Clean, Clean, Clean

In order to composite images together, there are several more steps beyond match lighting and eye-line considerations. You may choose to use visible rigs that need to be cleaned out or removed for final viewing. You may have some unwanted dirt or shadows that somehow crept into your shot and you want them out. There is a solution that is absolutely essential for this kind of cleaning and naturally it's called the "clean plate." The clean plate is a shot (often two or three frames) of the background set or image without the figure or moving object in the foreground of the frame. This clean plate needs to maintain the same lighting and background elements that you use during the animation. It is often shot just before the animation of your figure or object begins. For safety, it's smart to shoot a second clean plate just after you finish the animation (after removing the foreground image or figure). This approach is based on the camera being in a "locked down" or static position. If there is a camera move, then that exact same camera move has to be repeated to get all the appropriate clean-plate frames that the original shot provided without the animated object in the frame. This is where an accurate and stable computer-controlled motion-control unit can come into play. This machine should be able to repeat the move with accuracy if nothing has been moved other than the animated object. There is one more tedious approach to moving clean plates that you can use when you do not have motion control. This takes very exacting work. If you animate an object, move the camera, and then shoot, you must carefully remove the animated object from the frame and shoot the clean plate. You must put your object back into the frame, often using the onionskin option for proper placement, and then animate it again, repeating this process. If you are not careful and patient with this process then you will be more prone to making animation mistakes (Figure 10.7).

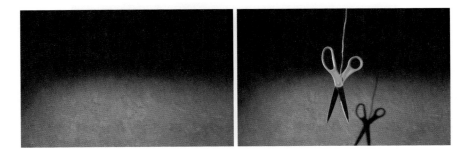

Figure 10.7

A shot of a clean plate next to the same composition with a foreground element.

Your support rig should have a minimum of junctions with the animated object or person. Ideally, you only want one intersection of the support rig and the animated object. This will make the cleanup go much faster. If your object is near a wall or someplace where the animated object casts a shadow, then you want to make sure that during the shooting the rig does not cross the shadow area of the animated object. The shadow will be very difficult to replace because the clean plate does not have the same shadow in it (Figures 10.8 and 10.9).

Figure 10.8

The ideal rig support placement.

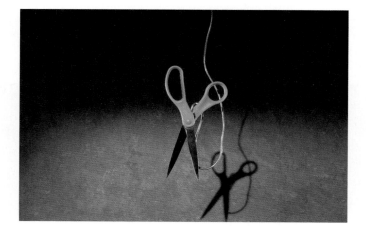

Figure 10.9

Too many junctions with the rig and object, with the rig covering the object shadow.

10. Collage (The Digital Advantage)

There are several ways and programs to clean rig supports, but in order to get the principle across I will use Photoshop as the demonstration tool. Programs like After Effects are ideal for this kind of work because they utilize the power of layering from Photoshop, but they do it more efficiently in a timeline. If you captured your animated scene on a flash card or in a program like Dragonframe, then you will have all of your shots in a folder sequentially numbered. Dragonframe will export these images to a QuickTime movie, but you will have to import the images from a flash card to a program like Final Cut or Premiere. Before you make your final movie from the scene, you will have to remove those cumbersome rigs. This has to be done frame by frame. In Photoshop, there are some shortcuts you can use, like "batch" processing frames. In the new extended version of Photoshop you can import QuickTime and image sequences. There is a timeline in this Photoshop that allows you to work on individual frames in a sequence. Ultimately, this is a slow, meticulous process and requires careful scrutiny on a frame-by-frame basis. No matter what approach you take, the goal is to place the clean plate on every animation frame that has a rig or cleanup issue as a background layer. It can be helpful to use a rig support that has a different color than your model so the delineation of the two elements is easier to distinguish. Carefully erase the rig and rig shadows of the animation frame on the top layer, revealing the clean plate behind it. These should match in placement, color, and light. I will often use a small, slightly feathered eraser at the interface point of the rig and animated object being supported. It is possible to use a larger feathered eraser for the rest of the rig because the rest of the rig is less critical in its placement (Figure 10.10).

Figure 10.10

The eraser tool wiping out a rig.

Once all of your frames have been cleaned, which should include any camera dirt or burnt-out pixels from the image sensor, you want to reexport those new frames to a QuickTime movie. Often you won't see some of the subtle imperfections in a shot until you see it in "running time." You may have to go back and address those problems for the particular frames that need additional work.

The Chroma Key

Chroma keying is becoming more prevalent in stop motion because it allows an animator to work with individual components or objects separately in any shot. This often saves space and massive set building. There are many uses for chroma keying so I asked Jeff Sias, who, along with his partner Bryan Papciak, runs a small studio in Boston called Handcranked Productions, to create a chroma key exercise that explains the process.

"Chroma keying" is a compositing term, meaning that anything of a particular color in frame will be eliminated through the process of "keying out" that color. If shooting with a green screen, then anything green in frame will be removed and become transparent. This allows you to composite your subject onto a new background. For this exercise, let's imagine that your subject is an animated flying saucer and you'd like to composite it into a real-life live-action night scene.

The first thing to do when planning a chroma keying shot is to determine what color you will be using as a keyable background. The typical keying colors are pure, saturated, and evenly lit green and blue because those are the colors least present in human skin tones. It is important to pick a screen color that is not part of your subject so that your key will be nice and clean. For example, if the flying saucer is silver and has a blue stripe around it, you will want to use a green screen background so that you don't lose the blue stripe in the keying process.

The next step is to plan the movement and animation of your subject. Remember that once you key out the background color, your subject can be moved around the frame freely, scaled and rotated however you like. You can animate the saucer hovering and spinning in center frame, but plan to animate and scale its larger movement as part of the compositing process within After Effects.

Using a two layer multiplane downshooter, you will set up the lower plane as the green screen with the saucer animating on the top glass plane. For the green screen background, use a solid tone super-saturated green card or cloth. Focus the camera lens on the saucer; you can let the background go out of focus, which will actually help the green screen key better. Think carefully about the lighting of the flying saucer and the scene it will be compositing into. In this case, the flying saucer might be lit as if with soft blue moonlight.

Once animated, you must bring the frames into your editing program as an image sequence or QuickTime movie. With After Effects, you can import either a QuickTime movie or a folder of sequentially named images. Either way, you will end up with your animated saucer as a single clip, ready to key

10. Collage (The Digital Advantage)

and composite. You will also want to import your background footage of the night sky at this point too.

Once you set up a working sequence in After Effects, add your background footage as the bottom layer in your timeline and then your saucer footage on top of that. Select the top saucer layer and go to the menu item: Effects // Keying // Color Key. Once the Color Key effect is applied to your saucer layer, you must pick the color it will key. Click on the little eye dropper tool in the filter window and use it to pick the green color on the saucer layer. Pick a point fairly close to the saucer's edge, as this will give you the cleanest key. If you have a nice, evenly lit green screen, you should immediately see most of the green around the saucer disappear, revealing the background night sky layer below. Play with the Color Tolerance parameter until all of the green is gone. If you can't remove all the green, you can always create a simple "garbage matte" to remove the rest. The point is to get the edge of your saucer as clean as possible.

To make the composite of the saucer perfect, there are still a few more steps. First, play with the Edge Thin and Edge Feather parameters. These will affect the edges of your saucer matte and clean up any jaggy lines. It is important to soften the edges of the saucer slightly so it marries into the background better. You may also want to apply a De-spill effect, which will help to remove any green tinge or green reflections on your saucer.

Once you have a nice matte, you will likely want to apply a color correction filter to your Saucer layer. In this case, you'll want to darken the saucer, give it more contrast, and add a dark blue or purple cast to it. This will help it feel integrated into the dark night sky. Key-framing these color correction effects as the saucer "flies" through the scene will further enhance the illusion.

Let's do a simple animation of the saucer flying into frame, hovering for a few seconds, and then flying off. Use your animation skills to think about how the saucer would move into frame. All you have to do is set a few key frames so the saucer will start small, zoom into frame, hover for a few seconds, and then zoom off into the distance. All of this can be achieved with only a few position and scaling key frames. Because you animated a slight hovering motion on the downshooter, you will retain a nice stop-motion feel to the shot (Figure 10.11).

As a last note, you may want to click the motion blur button of the saucer layer. This will add a blur to the frames where your saucer is moving fast. This adds a touch of realism and really helps your saucer feel like it is integrated into the background.

As you get more comfortable with the chroma keying and compositing process, you can try other keying filters and color effects. Keying and compositing is a whole specialty in and of itself, with many different techniques and filters to try. But understanding the basic concept and keeping your green screen evenly lit will get you great and believable results very quickly. Many of the artists I have included in this second edition utilize the power of programs like After Effects. The hyperlapse/time-lapse artist Geoff Tompkinson talks about his approach:

Figure 10.11

An example of the flying saucer on the green screen and matted onto a background. (Courtesy of Handcranked Productions LLC, Waltham, MA.)

I shoot everything as perfectly as possible in camera. However, as hyperlapse is attempting to manually emulate what would conventionally need a full motion-controlled rig to achieve, it is rare for the result out of camera to be perfect. Normally far from it.

So post production stabilization of the sequence is vital. It is possible to achieve good results in some cases using automatic software solutions like the Warp Stabilizer in After Effects but more often than not I resort to manual frame by frame repositioning of frames to achieve the desired end result. Typically post production takes a lot longer than shooting.

Geoff Tompkinson

It is critical to make sure your footage is as good as it can be, as stated earlier. Planning, lighting, lens choice, eyeline, and overall quality of the image all are necessary elements for good postproduction work. When people say "we'll fix it in post," there really is a strong note of sarcasm, because any good filmmaker knows that you do have to have good footage and well-planned shots in order to achieve a successful composite or effect.

Corrie Parks, whose sand animation has gone to the "next level," uses numerous layers in After Effects to get a sand look in the animation but also to go beyond the basics of sand animation into a unique approach to enhance her frame-by-frame animation. I am sure she does a lot of testing and layer preparation in order to get the wonderful refined look that she has achieved in her films.

11

Massaging Frames in the Edit

Composite of a laptop flying in and attacking an old film cutter by Tom Gasek.

Working the Frames
Impossible Perfection
File Management
Playback

Working the Frames

We have finally come to one of the last stages in the filmmaking process: editing. We discovered that in animation much of this editing is done early on in the preproduction process. The animatic, which is the moving timeline of the storyboard, should be the guide for the final edit in any animated film. We claimed that animation is so labor-intensive that overshooting scenes is not an option. So unlike live-action filmmaking, animation has done a good bit of the postproduction decision-making before the last process begins. Yet there are many fine details that need attention at the editing stage, and this is what we'll address.

Some basic principles of shooting and editing need to be examined before we get into some of the specific frame-by-frame options for editing. When you are shooting out of sequence for a film, which is fairly common in filmmaking, it is critical to always check any footage that has already been shot that might sit on the timeline on either end of the shot you are about to animate. You might want to shoot out of sequence because several shots have the same setup, and by shooting those shots together you will save a lot of production time in the setup. If you don't examine all the shots already animated on either side of your current shot, then you may miss an opportunity to match the shots for action, lighting, prop consistency, and framing. This could create a lot of trouble in the final edit. A common practice is to work with your animatic as the base edit. Each time you complete a shot, you should replace the corresponding storyboard, drawing from the animatic with the final animation. This will force you to keep an eye on the bigger picture and make sure that your cuts are working together.

> If I'm playing with dialogue I have a rough measure of how long I need. I usually shoot the movements (especially the mouths) leaving lots of held frames and then adjust the timings in the editing room.
>
> **Terry Gilliam**

Terry Gilliam is referring to a technique that is common in these alternative stop-motion techniques, and that is the manipulation of individual frames. Oftentimes while in the middle of a shoot you may wonder about the length of a particular hold of an object or person. It is always best to overshoot frames and have the ability to remove extra frames in the edit process. In this case, Gilliam is overshooting lip-sync frames and adjusting the timing with the sound in the edit. A tendency with novice stop-motion animators is to shoot even increments of their subject, which in the end will lose any dynamic in movement. With no variation in the movement from frame to frame, the movement of an object or person will be robotic. This should ultimately be addressed in the shooting process, but if you change your mind about a particular movement or action then the edit room becomes your last chance to improve things without a reshoot. You can remove frames between key positions for speed and snappy actions, and you can repeat frames to make a hold last longer so the audience can have a brief moment to catch up. The issue with repeating frames, as mentioned earlier, is that it's best to repeat sequential hold frames to keep the movement from freezing in place. Holding a single frame is an option, although it is important to make sure the animation is set up for this by using ease frames before and after the freeze. Oftentimes using a technique referred to as "rock and rolling" is the best way to keep hold frames alive. You would use Frame 1 of a sequence, then Frame 2 and Frame 3, back to 2 and 1, then back up to 2 and 3, and so forth. This way any jumps in the movement can be avoided. But like Gilliam, you want to make sure to always shoot enough frames of a hold or certain action if you think you might extend or cut them later in the edit. Juan Pablo Zaramella uses freeze-frames for holds, and it works quite well, as can be seen in his film *HotCorn!* His dramatic facial expressions and good timing work very well with the frozen hold frames and the contrast of movement and hold frames make this animated short, fresh and snappy. There are very few hard and fast rules in animation, and it often takes certain creative types to break any existing "rules" to forge new and interesting ground (Figures 11.1 and 11.2).

One final solution to holding frames is a postproduction effects solution. If you need a hold in an unexpected area and you only have one frame to hold, then duplicating that frame in post is possible. Later in After Effects, you can add a "grain and noise" filter to that one single frame. These duplicate frames with added grain won't feel quite so static and out of place in running time. But randomly placing holds in the edit process often won't work because when the movement begins again there probably won't be an ease-in of the action in the next frame, so the animation will jump.

Jeff Sias from Handcranked Productions describes another way to deal with giving your animation more dynamic in the editing process:

> Editing programs also have the ability to "ramp" speeds and have variable time changes with an editing graph. This will allow you to really tweak a particular motion if necessary. Also related to this is the idea of "frame blending," as in if you stretch a shot out in time, you can have the program try to create new in-between frames, either by blending frames together, or by tracking pixels and actually creating brand new frames. The latter option can create strange and undesirable-digital artifacts, but it works well on normal and slow moving objects if you only lengthen the shot by 200%–300% or less.
>
> **Jeff Sias**

Here's an exercise that will give you an idea of the ability you have in the edit to improve your timing in an animated action in a frame-by-frame film. The one important element that you must consider when using this technique is what else is happening in the background of the shot that you are frame-manipulating. When you pull frames to add dynamic to a foreground object or person, how will the elimination of those frames affect the background or secondary action in the overall animation composition? Complexity in the overall composition with

Figure 11.1

Three images from *HotCorn!* by Juan Pablo Zaramella. (Courtesy of Juan Pablo Zaramella © 2011.)

Figure 11.2

Rock and rolling frames for a hold.

multiple objects or people may prevent you from pulling and adding frames in the editing process.

In Chapter 8 there is an exercise where you animate a person along a wall frame by frame with eases for approximately 1 second of animation. There are still holds at the head and tail of the shot. You will need to create this footage if you have not already shot it. The playback rate is 30 FPS. Create an image sequence from these shots and convert it into a QuickTime movie in QuickTime Pro. As I mentioned before, QuickTime 7 Pro is an extremely helpful investment. You can also import this footage into an editing program like Final Cut or Adobe Premiere. You can do this by either creating a QuickTime movie of the footage or by importing the individual frames from a folder after setting the still/freeze duration to 00:00:00:01 under Editing in the user preferences area of Final Cut.

Once you have the frames on the timeline, use the filmstrip mode so you can see the individual frames. Then enlarge the timeline so you can clearly see each frame. In the original exercise, there was a 15-frame hold at the head. Go eight frames into that hold and rock and roll Frames 9, 10, and 11 three times (i.e., Frame 8, 9, 10, 11, 10, 9, 10, 11, 10, 9, 10, 11, 10, 9, 10, 11, 12). Once you have completed this, then move into the movement frames. You have 15 forward movements, including eases shot on twos. Move into those frames and remove the two frames from the fourth movement forward, the sixth movement forward, the eighth movement forward, the ninth movement forward, the eleventh movement forward, and finally the thirteenth movement forward. Remember that you need to remove two frames for each of these movements because you shot on twos. Finally, make sure you remove any unwanted gaps between frames by right-clicking on the gap in Final Cut. Once you have completed this, render the footage and export it as a QuickTime movie.

When you compare the two QuickTime movies (the original and edited footage), you will see the effect of the rock and roll hold extension and the ability to change the animation dynamically in the edit. This type of editing manipulation goes all the way back to the Cinemagician, Georges Melies.

Impossible Perfection

There is no perfect solution to any one film. It is the imperfection that gives each piece its unique character, yet we, as artists, have a tendency to keep refining our artistic expression until we run out of time. Each film is a learning experience, even for the more advanced filmmaker, and it's important to take the lessons of each film, close the book on the old film, and move on. This liberating approach will allow you to continue to grow and experiment, and that is the essence of this kind of filmmaking. Having said this, there is much more you can do to refine each filmic experience in the edit.

If you have been shooting with a DSLR still camera, the chances are that your images are large enough to scale up in size without losing resolution, even in high-definition playback. This means that you can simulate simple camera moves in postproduction either in After Effects or a similar program or in Premiere. I prefer actual camera moves to simulated moves because real camera moves give you a genuine perspective change in the image that the post move does not. The post move just moves across the surface of the image. It does not penetrate the composition like a real camera move. There are times when a post-simulated move can be effective—for example, if you want a hand-held camera feel; if you are shooting flat images like photographs and you want to push in (and there would be no perspective change anyway); or if you just want to keep a scene alive with a subtle track. A digital move can augment a real physical move. However, generally postproduction moves done in these programs are effective if they are extreme or subtle, but they are less successful in the ground between.

Mixing live-action elements with single-frame footage takes a lot of planning. We covered match-lighting and object–person interaction in the previous chapter, but another element of this kind of composite work is adjusting the colors to match. If your white balance option was not set correctly in the shooting stage, then the edit is the time to correct this oversight. Thinking about an interesting color palette or plan is important in the planning stage but it is the post work that fine-tunes the differences that may occur in shooting. The bottom line is that you need to have good footage to begin with, but there is some latitude in color correction whether you do it in Premiere, Final Cut Pro, Photoshop, or After Effects. It's best to identify one establishing shot and color correct that shot to the best of your ability. All of the following shots should be matched to that default color-corrected master scene, usually a wide establishing shot. There is the possibility of changing the overall color palette in the postproduction process but usually this should have been explored in the preproduction stage. Your attitude and ideas do evolve during a film's development, so allowing yourself a chance to play with the colors in color correction is worth the time. You might change the image to black and white or a sepia tone; shift the contrast, saturation, brightness, and color scheme; or add filters to view your film in another perspective. Keep track of all the changes and their corresponding filter measurements so you can duplicate a look that you have discovered and want to apply to other parts of your film. You can accomplish this by saving your filters and effects settings as presets. This will allow you to reapply the same exact effect to any shot at any time.

File Management

Another important practice that needs to be sorted out in the preproduction stage is the naming convention for all of your files. If you establish a good file-naming system and stick with it, then the editing and post work will become much more manageable. There are several ways you can do this, but here is a system I used on my film *Off-Line.*

Title abbreviation = OL
Scene = sc
Take = t
Frame number = f
Effects = e
Final frames = F
You must consider the full range of scenes that are in your film and the maximum number of frames that are in any scene, and that number in the tens or hundreds will have to be carried out throughout.

"OLsc09t1f055eF"

This would be a final frame with effects. None of my shots had more than 999 frames in them, and my film had 99 scenes or less. This may seem like a long naming convention, but you can easily identify any frame in or out of place at any time.

There might be several drafts of effects that you apply to your frames and you might have to consider temporarily adjusting your naming convention to give you an idea where you are in the effects process. For example, if you have color corrected and cleaned out some rigs but have not composited additional images on your frames, then you might put a *d* after the *e* in your naming convention. The *d* would represent a certain *draft* or pass of the effects, so you could write *ed1* at the end and leave that in the overall effects folder until you finish the effects of those frames. When you complete the effects, just label the frame with an *e*, and perhaps it will be finished at that point so you can complete the naming convention with an *F* at the end. The important thing to remember is that you need to set this naming convention up early and keep it consistent for you and any crew that are working with you. Once again Jeff Sias weighs in about naming conventions.

It is important for After Effects to "see" a complete image sequence. If there are any missing numbers in the sequence, AE will assume that the frame is missing and replace it with a warning frame. You can also use a utility program, like Automator (on the Mac) to batch re-name the files in a sequence. Adobe Bridge also does a good job of batch re-naming, but Automator is faster.

Jeff Sias

Playback

We touched on frame rates when we explored pixilation. It's always best to decide and commit to a frame rate when you animate your material. There are so many things to consider with your playback rate, like how fluid do you want your animation, how much time do you have to shoot or animate, and how much finesse and control do you need in the movement of your object, person, or image? I like to shoot two frames per move at a playback rate of 30 FPS. I can also take one picture per movement and have a playback rate of 15 FPS. It is possible to slow down or speed up playback rates in editing programs like Premiere or Final Cut Pro, but I don't recommend speeding up or slowing down a shot more than 15%, especially when slowing down a shot. It often doesn't look as good, and the animation can have a more staccato look, which can be distracting. It is worth experimenting with frame rates to establish the playback pace and feeling that you want. Keep in mind that After Effects can process your frames with "frame blending," which essentially is creating in-between frames when you slow down your footage. This can make a big difference in the playback. Anytime you have a camera move, it is essential to shoot on single frames for a move that is fluid and not jerky. If you shoot a camera move on "singles," then it is best to animate your subjects at 30 FPS (one move for each of those 30 FPS) as well. Otherwise you might get a strobing quality between the camera move and the subject movement.

One old trick that many filmmakers use effectively is playing footage backwards. It can have a very interesting effect. Images or objects can appear to assemble themselves or perform unnatural movements. If you follow the normal laws of physics like recoil, inertia, and momentum with the idea of playing a scene backwards, then you will have a very successful effect. Another reason for a reverse playback would be if you are animating to a final position or graphic that would be very difficult to achieve animating frame by frame forward. In this case, you shoot the final frame in its predetermined and finessed position, take it apart frame by frame, and then reverse the playback (Figures 11.3 and 11.4).

One habit that you should consider when shooting any animation that will help in the editing process is shooting "handles." This basically means that you should shoot an extra 5–10 frames at the head and tail of each shot, even though you might have a very closely timed animatic. These extra frames will give you a little more freedom on the actual cut point in the edit and it will give you more footage if you have to vary the speed of your playback. Ideally these additional head and tail frames should be animated.

One issue that does arise from different sources is flicker or fluctuation in the overall animated image during playback. We discovered in Chapter 5 about cinematography that small variations in the iris of certain lenses or variations in the power source that powers your lights could cause minor exposure fluctuations. There are some solutions to this flicker effect. These postproduction solutions will not resolve overall fluctuations due to moving shadows and shifting light sources but will even out overall image variation. It is always best to first use appropriate lenses, like manual lenses that don't open and close the iris, and try to filter your power if you want a nice even exposure on all of your shots. But if you can't achieve this, then it's time to turn to a program like After Effects. If you open up Effects // Color Correction // Color Stabilizer and look for the Set Frame button

Figure 11.3

An animated image that needs art direction and should be animated backwards.

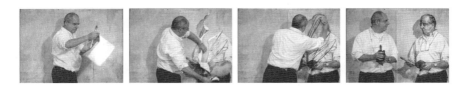

Figure 11.4

William Kentridge playing his footage backwards to have artwork appear to assemble itself with the guidance of Kentridge. "Invisible Mending." (Courtesy of Marian Goodman Gallery, New York, and The Goodman Gallery, Johannesburg, South Africa.)

in the attributes area, then you can establish the color reference frame. You can set the reference frame through brightness adjustment, levels, or curves. You may have to set a new reference frame, depending on the activity in the frame or if there is a camera move. Breaking the shot up into multiple sections and then reassembling the sections can solve any difficulties of having to set a new reference frame. This is not a perfect solution but can help. There are more effective After Effects plug-ins that do the job, but they are more expensive as solutions to overall image flutter. Filters and names change with each upgrade so I would

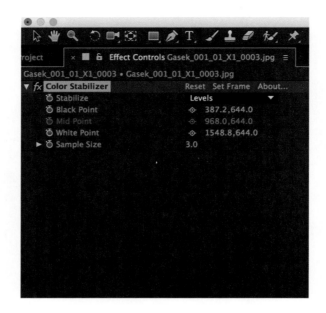

Figure 11.5

The Color Stabilizer menu in After Effects.

advise searching for the terms "flicker" and/or "fluctuation" in the help or search menu of any forum or program that deals with these kinds of issues (Figure 11.5).

Editing is an important and deep art form in the filmmaking process. There are many books written on the subject, including Michael Ondaatje's *The Conversations: Walter Murch and the Art of Editing Film*, Murch's *In The Blink of an Eye*, and *On Film Editing* by Edward Dmytryk. Animation is one form of filmmaking, and it should be treated in a similar manner to live-action editing when it comes to cutting pace and flow. Using techniques like "cutting on the action," dissolves for a passage of time, "jump cutting" for a jarring effect, and dynamic pacing in the overall cut are critical to all filmmaking, even frame-by-frame animation.

12

Exposure to the Market

Portrait of Jan Svankmajer. (Courtesy of Jan Svankmajer and Jaromir Kallista. © 2010. Athanor Ltd. Film Production Company, Jaromir Kallista, and Jan Svankmajer.)

The resources I use to implement my plan are determined by the subject. Never vice versa.

I would advise young filmmakers that they not copy or follow anyone but go their own way ....

Jan Svankmajer

Now What?

Once your project is complete, you will most likely want to share it with others and let the film develop a life of its own. It's rare to sit back and let the film capture its own audience. You have to promote it and expose it, and then the snowball can start to roll. If you had a particular audience in mind when you created your film, then that starts to focus your postproduction marketing. There are many venues these days and lots of competition for those venues, so it's important to be stealthier about where you want your film to flourish. Many filmmakers are more than happy to immediately post their original work to the World Wide Web. The exposure they get on the Web can be far better than any other approach. Film festivals are another means of exposure. They are not always easy to get into, and they often have application fees associated. European festivals tend not to have fees, but festivals in the United States usually do. They can elevate the perception of your film because they are juried. Taking this route requires some research and good choices. Commissioned work is another venue that already has its audience and special requirements, but there can be some wonderful creativity and freedom in this form. This might include commercials, informational and educational formats, webisodes, or even music videos. Finally, some filmmakers are strictly creating and producing for themselves, often in an experimental mode, and they may not care if many people see these experiments. Since they are filmmakers, I would imagine that they do want an audience, but it may be in a more nontraditional film venue like a gallery, a nightclub, or an exclusive screening at an event.

The bottom line is that you do whatever you can to help your film find an audience, and sometimes that approach takes unexpected turns and direction. Several of the artists I have cited in this book weighed in with the comments below:

The BBC brought Monty Python to the world—we never thought of an intended audience—and I tagged along. Now we just market recycled Python. People still buy.

Terry Gilliam

Mostly, when I create a short or an independent work I'm not trying to market it. I make it because I want to or I want to share a story or a feeling. Or honestly, I often want to try a new technique or am bored and want to create.

Lindsay Berkebile

We choose a song that we like and inspires us with visual ideas or a story. We believe that if you do something that you like other people will like it too. Then the profitable work will come.

Yuval Nathan

The films are sold through art galleries, and are seen primarily in art exhibitions. They are almost never shown on TV, and very occasionally in film festivals. Mostly they are shown in art galleries or museums.

William Kentridge

My films reached an audience of people like me and my friends, probably in an educational setting or via TV broadcast. The beauty of the National Film Board is that it doesn't aim for a mass market though it does have a responsibility to the Canadian taxpayers who fund it.

Carolyn Leaf

We don't really put a lot of energy into marketing our work. We believe if we create something of value the audience will spread it for us. On the flip side, if we don't create something of value it will die a silent death online. Even though we try really hard, we recognize that not everything we produce will be brilliant. The audience is the best judge of what works and our goal is just to help them share some laughs.

Evan Spiridellis

I marketed my work for a world-wide audience, I suspected little kids might get a bit scared but I've been proved wrong and the film has been made available for education—from India to Israel to Europe and the USA. I marketed my work through making posters for each festival we got in to (over 100) worldwide; the screenings and awards resulted in Stanley Pickle getting distribution on iTunes and Amazon as well as being made available in education through Into Film run by the British Film Institute (BFI). The British Council have taken the film all over the world to share with many diverse audiences as an example of British animation from Scotland to Papua New Guinea. Stanley Pickle was also screening on flights from the UK to LA for about a year.

Victoria Mather

Record and Archive the Process

It has become more critical these days to document each frame-by-frame project that you produce. Even for small short experiments, documentation can be very helpful as a record or notebook of the details of each experience. There are many very good reasons to record your process. I find when I'm in the heat of a shoot I really don't want to break to take pictures of what I am doing, but it's important to include this activity in your preproduction schedule. If you ever publish your work on a DVD or website, then including some documentation of the process will add depth and interest to your film project. We are so visually centered as a culture, and there is a lot of sophistication in our understanding of films. Audiences often have as much interest in the process as they do the final film. Many young filmmakers are keeping blogs that record their progress on a frame-by-frame production. This allows people who might be vested in their project through fund-raising programs like Kickstarter or Indiegogo to follow the progress of your film and stay involved. It builds a great relation between the investor and production group. Often there are opportunities for viewers to comment on the production progress, giving filmmakers a broader perspective on their creation. Early "objective" feedback can be critical to making any appropriate adjustments to your film. These blogs should be updated on a regular basis with photographs, short animated clips, and written notes, potentially with an opportunity for that all-important feedback. I want to take a quick moment to write about feedback on your film. It can be difficult to change work that you have already produced because viewers are saying "it's not working," but naturally the earlier you get this feedback, the better you will be in the overall production. If your film is for a particular audience, then you want them to connect to the film. Sometimes filmmakers cannot see the problems because we are so "close" to the work and filmmaking, especially animation, is too laborious to produce and not use. Sometimes feedback is not in line with what you, the filmmaker, want to say, so you make the ultimate decision. If you are getting the same kind of feedback from various sources, then it is worth considering seriously.

The other advantage of documenting your work is having a deeper and fuller understanding of your own work process. This is a valuable resource for you when it comes to explaining to others how you work. You may have to educate a potential client in the process of your work before they seriously consider giving you a commission. It also can guide you in potentially making a bid for a job that utilizes a similar technique for a commissioned work. The more you understand how you work and what process you need to complete that work, the more you can reasonably make a bid for a job that has a certain budget and schedule. You may have to hire help to produce a commissioned work, and you will need to be smart about how long you need that help for. If you know how long a particular process takes, like drawing out a storyboard, then you know how long you need a storyboard artist and you can multiply that number by the pay rate you offer the storyboard artist. In your documentation of each film, you should not only consider the visual recording process (e.g., stills and video), but you should also keep a notebook with brief notes about where to get certain materials, notes about locations and events that may occur during your shoot, how long you estimated for an event, and how long it actually took. This information and visual record keeping can be a wonderful way to present your independent film work at festivals, lectures, and tours, let alone benefit your own future productions.

Websites and the Internet

Sites like YouTube and Vimeo host most films free of charge, but it is important to understand the rules of how they work. Once you put something on the net, it virtually becomes public property. I don't mean this literally. You should still own the copyright of your film, although some sites may have some ownership claim as long as you are using their services. Always read the rules of any service that you utilize. The other option is to pay for a service that hosts your particular website and you can post your own work on your own site. Films can be downloadable or not. You make the choice. I have a personal website that hosts my main pages and small commercial clips of animation. Some pages have links to noncommercial work on Vimeo, and I have a link to a free blog service so I can interact with my site on a regular basis. There are all sorts of combinations and you have to find something that suits your needs and ability.

Short films don't have many revenue-making venues, but this doesn't stop independent animators from producing. If you're interested in making money on your work, then you need to invest in yourself by producing original work that becomes a calling card for your particular services. Once you get your work out into the world (and the net is great for that kind of low-cost exposure), then people will see your work and may approach you with commissioned work (which is often similar to the original work that you posted on the net). It's the offshoots of your original work that make the money, and the original work serves as a promotional investment. Some artists feel that posting their work online (especially on their own sites) fosters an interest in viewers to own a hard copy of your film, so DVDs are sold through fee services like PayPal, which can be linked to your site. If you really want the world to see your work, then it helps to have short, clever, and inexpensive ideas that you are willing to produce with little or no payback. Opportunities can arise for exclusive showings of your work for a fee to you, but usually this doesn't happen when your work is on the web. This is why filmmakers try to get into festivals before posting work on the web. The exposure is limited at these festivals, and so showing your film at more festivals or broadcast venues becomes more attractive for distributors. There are a growing number of websites that will host your work in a nonexclusive manner with other similar work, like children's animation and so on. These sites package your film with others and sell them, with some small revenue coming back to you, but this is best if you own all the rights to your film, music included. Otherwise it becomes more complicated and not worth the small return.

Film Festivals

The film festival is the traditional way to get your animated film out into the world. You not only show your film at these festivals but you meet people from around the world with similar interests and different approaches to filmmaking. Both experienced and novice animators and fans attend these festivals, and these people are generally pretty accessible for conversations. Seeing what other filmmakers are producing can be very inspiring. Exchanging ideas with people who are driven to make animated films, with all of the struggle that can be related, can help your morale when you feel defeated by the big commitment that frame-by-frame filmmaking can require. Sometimes these festivals are where you will find commissioned work or even potential distribution for your film.

There is a lot involved in this process and it takes constant research and follow-through. Fortunately, there are many new tools and websites that help make this process much more efficient and easy to navigate. In my experience, two of the most widely accepted sites are Withoutabox and FilmFreeway. Hundreds of festivals, primarily in the United States but also around the world, accept film submissions through these sites. You basically fill out a thorough application form for each and every film you want to send out into the world, and you can even upload your film to these sites for festival jury viewing, so that you save lots of time and money. These festivals will look at the websites' generic application and view your online viewing copy or "screener" of the film. You have the option of sending a screening copy to the festivals directly even though you have submitted your application through these sites, or you can upload a high-resolution copy for special download by the festivals. Now that there is more competition in this arena, the fees associated have been reduced, which is helpful to independent filmmakers. You are given a reference number so the screening copy can be matched to the application when it arrives at the festival if you send a copy in the mail (Figures 12.1 and 12.2).

Choosing the appropriate festivals is very important. Many festivals will require that you not have your film online if they show it at their festival. This makes their festival appear more exclusive and interesting to attend. For this reason, many filmmakers don't put their complete film online (only teaser clips) until at least one full cycle of festivals has run its course, which is usually about 2 years. Your best chance of getting into a festival is when you choose to premiere your film at that festival, so it's important to make the right choice. Many frame-by-frame stop-motion productions fall into a few categories like "animation," "narrative," "experimental," "music video," and so on, but do not limit your festival choices to animation festivals exclusively. Many festivals have themes and agendas like "films and technology," "American documentaries," or "new directors," so it's important to read about these festivals before you enter. Withoutabox and FilmFreeway will put you on their mailing list once you join up, and you will be able to research

Figure 12.1

The Withoutabox home page.

12. Exposure to the Market

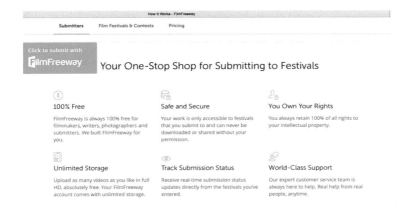

Click to submit with

FilmFreeway   Your One-Stop Shop for Submitting to Festivals

100% Free

FilmFreeway is always 100% free for filmmakers, writers, photographers and submitters. We built FilmFreeway for you.

Safe and Secure

Your work is only accessible to festivals that you submit to and can never be downloaded or shared without your permission.

You Own Your Rights

You always retain 100% of all rights to your intellectual property.

Unlimited Storage

Upload as many videos as you like in full HD, absolutely free. Your FilmFreeway account comes with unlimited storage.

Track Submission Status

Receive real-time submission status updates directly from the festivals you've entered.

World-Class Support

Our expert customer service team is always here to help. Real help from real people, anytime.

Figure 12.2

The FilmFreeway home page.

these festivals through the sites' steady updates. It might be important to submit to a festival that is near where you live so you can attend the festival, or you might consider a local regional festival, which will be to your advantage. Most festivals will not pay for your expenses getting to the festival, even when you are a potential winner. They usually will give you a free pass, but often that's as far as it goes. There are some exceptions, and this is why it's important to do your research. Big festivals like Sundance, South by Southwest, Annecy, and many of the urban international festivals are a good place to try and premiere your film because other festival programmers go to these festivals—they may see your film and ask you later to submit to their festival (often waiving entry fees).

Getting into a festival means that some experienced and seasoned filmmakers and people associated with the business have chosen your film over dozens and often hundreds or thousands of other films to show at their festival. The juries on the larger festivals have a fair amount of credibility, so that gives your film a thumbs-up as it enters the public arena. Just getting into a festival in today's competitive atmosphere is a great accomplishment. If you don't get into a particular festival, it does not necessarily reflect badly on your film. The competition is very high since filmmaking is so much more accessible than it used to be, and often your film may not fit the theme, agenda, or style of film that a particular jury is seeking. Keep trying to find a festival venue for your film by starting high and working your way down into the lesser-known festivals. The fees associated with entering a festival can start to drain your account, so start and enter early to save money with "early bird specials," and consider calling up the festival directly if you are broke and ask for an entry fee waiver. You just might get it.

You should expect that you won't make any money on your short film, but it might get you some recognition that can be translated into revenue in the form of a commission. Some people do get lucky and are approached by film distributors and director representatives. The latter will represent you in the commercial world for a commission, which can vary depending on how involved they become in your future projects. There are many possibilities and, if you are approached, remember that it's best to get information about what is being offered and don't make any fast decisions. If one distributor approaches you, then most likely more will come. The deals that are offered may include exclusive screenings on television or the Internet for a period of time in certain markets. Other offers may include being part of a collection of animated shorts that will be screened and distributed internationally or placed on a website that has large exposure with the potential for future sales (although this last revenue source can be pretty miniscule). There are numerous opportunities on the web that offer some revenue. Remember that you can market and sell your own films, but revenue may be limited by the lack of exposure that some of these commercial opportunities can offer. People involved in promotion and distribution are constantly scanning the web at sites like YouTube and Vimeo looking for new talent. Vimeo even has a "short of the week" or "staff picks" endorsement, which boosts the exposure and credibility of your animated short. If your short is posted on a site that has a built-in audience and your animated short receives thousands of hits or viewings, then you can be sure that your film is being seen by people who may be able to offer you opportunities to make some money. You must be careful about the opportunities that come through these routes, since they vary in range and there is little or no regulation. People can contact you through sites like Vimeo, Facebook, and LinkedIn, so you are sure to see some action.

Ownership

The current copyright laws protect any filmmaker the moment they create and produce any film. It is required that you "publish" your work or just have some way to prove when you produced this film. It is important to print your name with the copyright symbol (©) next to it and the year you completed the film as your final frame (Figure 12.3).

This is also true for the preproduction script, drawings, and layouts. Since some sites do have restrictions about ownership, when you post on them it might be best to post your film work on your own site so there is no misunderstanding. You also have some other options with this kind of posting.

Some filmmakers utilize the Creative Commons option, which allows others to use their work under very specific conditions but for no fee. These conditions might include educational or noncommercial venues that allow their work to be exposed to a greater audience and with the possibility for the work to become part of a larger communal production. Music can also fall into the Creative Commons category if so stated by the copyright holder.

If you feel that you want to have "rock solid" protection, then you might think of registering your images, script, and branding with the US copyright office.

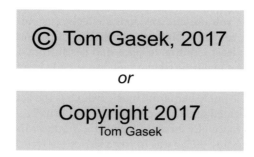

© Tom Gasek, 2017

or

Copyright 2017
Tom Gasek

Figure 12.3

An example of the copyright statement that should be at the end of every film.

This can be done online by visiting their site at www.copyright.gov. You can find out everything you need to know about ownership and protection of your creative products on this government site. "Orphan works" legislation seems to hit Congress every so often, threatening the protection of all creative ideas and output in a tangible medium like photography and other visual mediums. The advantage to this legislation is that it would offer producers access to use artistic tangible mediums that don't appear to have copyright holders, like old photographs, recordings, and images. The danger is that this legislation can be applied to more contemporary work that appears to have no copyright owner, mostly because many of these images and tangible mediums don't have author/artist identification associated with them. With the advent of the web and the proliferation of images and ideas, this legislation could move down a slippery path to exploitation of ideas and images by producers who don't make intensive efforts to identify and notify authors of the use of their creative work by others. The Library of Congress wants to move the burden of finding authors to private databases in the area of the artwork, which starts to lose the regulation of a central authority. It will be interesting to see where this legislation goes, and it's worth watching. This will affect both national and international use of images and ideas and is a difficult issue to easily resolve.

One last word about ownership and copyright. Music is an art form that demands as much respect as any visual art form. We said earlier that sound should be half of the picture. If you have commissioned music for your animated film, then make sure you have an agreement with the composer to give all rights (exclusive or nonexclusive) to you for the use of the music with your film "in perpetuity." When I commission a specific piece of music for my film, I require a "buyout" of the music so that there is no problem with potential future sales. I even insist that the music be named after the film for identification purposes. This approach usually costs the most but prevents future problems. You can pay less if you can use the music for your film in perpetuity but others can use the music as well, if they find an appropriate match. Ultimately you *must* clear the rights to any music you use *and* any sound effects, custom-made or not. If you don't do this, then you are robbing the musicians of potential revenue, and you could be sued or at least required to cease and desist from using the music right away. This could be a major problem if you are already in a festival mode. If you use existing music, then you must search out the ownership both from the author of the music and the publisher of the music (which is the actual recording). This can be very complicated and time-consuming and usually requires a significant amount of money, especially for an independent producer like yourself. One way I decided to use existing music was to pay a fee for festival rights for 2 years and then the right to put the animated short up online for promotional nonprofit exposure in perpetuity. This costs less than getting the ultimate rights for the music for the entire life of the film. Festival rights are a good initial start to see if the film does well, and if it does then you can renegotiate further rights with the publishers and authors down the road. If the film slowly fades away in the festival world, then you have not spent too much on getting ultimate rights for the music.

A Few Thoughts

This book is intended for both the novice and more experienced filmmaker, but I want to address the beginners in these alternative stop-motion techniques. It's important in the early stages of making these kinds of films to keep things fresh and not overly controlled. Each film should be treated like a sketch and not a masterpiece that reflects high craft. Allow yourself to make "mistakes" and take risks. Although I have cited some specific approaches to these techniques, as I have mentioned, there really are no hard and fast rules. Keep your ideas simple and manageable so you can accomplish them. Shoot for small goals within your reach. Don't overcomplicate your idea. The process will automatically get complicated with all the problem-solving that you will encounter, so keeping your idea simple will work in your favor.

If you are interested in learning more about how stop-motion studios and artists operate, then consider making some short experiments—put together a reel of your best work and start researching who is making these kinds of films and making a living or even just getting publicity for these kinds of productions. The Internet is a wonderful research tool, especially if you follow sites like awn.com and cartoonbrew.com and see what is going on in the industry. Contact these people and ask if you can show your work and get some feedback from them. The issue of internships might enter the conversation, but just getting a little of these artists' time and seeing how they operate is worth the effort. You will find that many of these artists are just driven to produce these animated film shorts. Many times there is not much money involved. That displays the passion that is necessary to work in this area. If you are fortunate enough to get some commissioned work, like a commercial or a short informational film, then consider it an opportunity to experiment and push the bounds, within reason. Your client will want to know what you will produce, but there should still be a chance to step out a bit and try something fresh and new. Don't forget to allow yourself "testing" time. It will pay off.

These techniques open up a wide range of possibilities for established and potential new filmmakers. As I mentioned in the Introduction, the moving image is becoming more and more accessible to a larger pool of producers. Live-action filmmakers want to stylize their films, and this is one way that is not totally foreign to them, since the use of photography, lighting, and performance are involved in both approaches. You really don't need to know how to draw or sculpt well, but you do have to have good ideas and some skills, and these frame-by-frame techniques are a great way to add something new and different to live-action. This is also true for photographers who are now using DSLR still cameras that have the capability to shoot high-definition video. These photographers will want to know how to take advantage of these camera assets. I have tried to incorporate a few basic animation techniques and principles in these chapters as well as describe what frame-by-frame artists are now producing without getting too technical. The associated website will have many technical hints and approaches, which are always changing with technology, but the fundamentals are described in these chapters.

If you start to think about the infinite combinations and possibilities in this area, you can get overwhelmed. Just about anything can be animated to serve an idea. Some things are easier to animate and control than others, and keeping this in mind when you chose an object or person will help determine the result that you get. It is important to apply tried and true animation techniques and principles to your movement to elicit a dynamic result. Pixilation that has some snap and punch will be more interesting to watch than evenly paced movement. Time-lapse that is dynamic in composition, contains contrast, and has dynamic transformation can be fascinating. You must understand the time-lapse subject first before you commit it to film. This way you will get the best angle, you will understand the best part of an event to record, and you can be prepared for the change that will occur in front of the camera. As we have seen, the postproduction side of time lapse and the other frame-by-frame techniques have opened up an even larger pallet to explore, partly through extensive post work. Downshooting or using a multiplane animation stand can be a rich art form when used with cutouts, sand, three-dimensional objects, or an infinite range of material. The ability to shoot in a "down and dirty" approach, which can be fast and fresh-looking, is really appealing to some filmmakers. This art form also has the ability to be subtle and refined with its multilayer look, whether this is executed practically or in postproduction. It has the advantage of the photographic approach, and look and objects generally don't have to fight gravity, the eternal bane of stop-motion animators. I hope you consider playing with these techniques. They can be fairly fast to produce and very satisfying in their results. These techniques can be a sketchbook approach to animation or a refined and beautiful expression of art. Enjoy these techniques and have fun, because that will show in your work.

I leave you with a few more statements and advice from some of the filmmakers that we cited throughout the previous chapters. Shoot on …

If I have any guiding principle regarding the stop frame process, it's to try and accommodate or embrace any spontaneous ideas that might present themselves during the animation. Stop frame is generally a long, slow process and unless one is unduly preoccupied with the more laborious requirements of a shot, additional and peripheral ideas are always going to occur.

Dave Borthwick

Focus on what you have that makes your work unique.

Yuval Nathan

Start filming immediately. Understand that every part of the work is a self-portrait. This can be either dispiriting, or reassuring.

William Kentridge

My approach to time-lapse is very organic. I don't over-think or over-plan my shots. I go 90% by instinct; the other 10% is just making sure the logistics are in place to support the first 90%. The subjects of my time-lapse sequences also appeal to me greatly—outdoor and astronomy subjects, which bring me to the most spectacular and inspiring natural locations I can find. For me, this beats sitting in a studio ten hours a day.

Tom Lowe

Embrace the tech, but remember the basics of image-making. Technology is the means, not the end!

Eric Hanson

I gave up cut-out animation because it is easier to achieve emotions with live action filming and I don't have the patience to do beautiful full animation. The fact is, I always wanted to be film director … animation was an interesting detour.

Terry Gilliam

Play around with the material and see what kind of images you can make and move. Don't expect the kind of control you can get from computer imagery. Make images that please you to look at, and you will find that you have the patience to move them.

Carolyn Leaf

Finally, I understood that, like Bob Dylan said, sometime, someplace, "to live outside the law, you must be honest." By this I mean that I intended, finding myself suddenly in this big, intimidating and

typically controlling industry, to continue to "live outside the law."
I wanted to make the videos my way, and to be trusted to look out for
the interests that had been entrusted in us and to repay that trust in spades, to "be
honest"—To deliver something more valuable than anyone could have anticipated,
including us. Not to mention, on schedule at every juncture and on budget.

Jim Blashfield

Life is too short to make a film that takes two years being unhappy with the result.
I'm getting older, I do not have dreams of success, only dreams of films. Sometimes
you miss your goal, but you did your best. That's something I can accept. Don't
start a project knowing you are going to get a bad picture.

Jan Kounen

I like to stay grounded and come from a base of balance and spaciousness when
I am working. I have a cozy studio in an old warehouse near the Willamette
River. I love my work and I am excited to get to the studio every morning.

Joanna Priestley

Pick up a camera, or your phone, download a stop motion app and try it out with
a friend. Laughter is guaranteed, but whatever you do, don't laugh! For those more
serious about making a film using this technique, test it out and see if you can
bring something new to it. Making a carbon copy of something that already exists
is pointless—bring something new to the conversation to ensure that it evolves and
doesn't repeat.

Victoria Mather

The best advice I could give would be to try *everything*. There is no right or wrong
way to do this stuff. People should read and take in whatever advice and information they can find but ultimately they should distill it all and find their own way
to do it. The only other advice I could give would be to work your A$$ off!!! If
you don't absolutely love this stuff you are better off finding another career. Look
for something that you love so much you can't stop talking, thinking and dream-
ing about it. My guess is if you are reading this book you are probably passionate
enough to give it a run!

Evan Spiridellis

PRO-File James (Jamie) Caliri and Dyami Caliri

Jamie Caliri. (Courtesy of Jamie Caliri.)

JC: I have been working professionally as an animation director since 1989.

TDG: Please describe the relationship between your *Dragon* spot for United and the software that you created.

JC: I worked for years shooting on 35-mm film for all of my projects. In 2005 I was directing a commercial for United Airlines called *Dragon*— we looked into shooting with digital still cameras. As the project started, we started making a simple application to give the animators a way to frame flip. As we moved through the shoot we kept adding features like multiple exposures and line up images and movies. We also added the camera move calculator that we had in our old Apple 2E program. It was a few more years to realize we should see if anyone else wanted to use our system. We released the software to the public in 2008.

JC: I design the user interface and guide the development of the software. My brother Dyami is the lead software engineer. He also lends a hand in design. We discuss and work through every feature. We have a unique set of complementary skills and we enjoy making this software.

Dyami Caliri at the computer. (Courtesy of Jamie Caliri.)

TDG: One of the unique qualities of Dragonframe is that it interfaces with DSLR cameras. When and how did you decide that this was the kind of camera that would be the future of stop motion?

JC: If only I could take credit for this one. The United commercial was shot on a high end point and shoot made by Leica. It was a Leica Digilux 2. Later it would be the animator Tennessee Norton Reid that encouraged us to take notice of the soon-to-be-released DSLRs from Canon and Nikon. He clued us in and pushed us to release the software (send him a thank-you note if you like Dragonframe).

Close-up of a camera shooting "Dragon" for United Airlines. (Courtesy of Jamie Caliri © 2007.)

TDG: Dragonframe has developed dramatically over the last 7 or 8 years. What do think are the biggest improvements?

JC: Hmm—I would say overall stability is the most important quality to be strengthened over time. We see a lot of studios using our DMX dimmer program workspace. Also we keep improving our audio track reading. Motion control is a huge addition, although only the big studios seem to take advantage of that.

In Dragonframe 2 we introduced the keypad controller. That is very useful and it is exciting to see how people use it.

We don't really include editing features and we don't want to make people think they should edit at all in DF. We do have frame editing within a shot to help with getting your shot just right. This also helps with creating holds and repeated cycles.

TDG: Please address the expansion into motion control. Why was this important and do you supply your own motion-control hardware?

JC: When Dragonframe controls the camera with our DMC-16 it makes shooting quite smooth. Dragonframe can take the animator back in time if they have to cut back. We automatically take out any backlash from the system. With our Virtual programing space you can import 3D moves made in Maya. Virtual will be in Dragonframe 4.

Jamie working at a *Dragon* set with motion control. (Courtesy of Jamie Caliri.)

TDG: Please discuss your Dragonframe blog and website and what you want to achieve with your well-supported website.

JC: When we started the blog we just wanted to let potential software buyers know other filmmakers were making great work with it. Now we are just excited to share fun videos. We try to have a new blog posted every Monday with a fun creative film to feature.

TDG: What is the future of Dragonframe?

JC: We will add a bell to remind you to go outside and play Frisbee with your friends and family. Actually, we try to keep up with all of the great ideas from the field. Animators use a lot of video reference these days. They often have live-action video of themselves or the director acting out moments. We are working on making the process of loading, organizing, and viewing those video much easier. We love making Dragonframe. It's exciting to try and make the art of stop motion a bit easier for everyone.

TDG: When I asked Dyami about Dragonframe 4, here's what he had to say. DF4 will have movie recording on some cameras that support it (Canon EOS, Nikon, Sony). So you can capture live video, perhaps with a live camera move (if you have a DMC-16), and then animate the same move in stop motion.

There have always been numerous stop motion programs for computers and webcams. The phone apps are similar in that they are great for playing around. I don't see them as a real competitor for our software, because you *can't realistically do professional work with them.* And we don't have any need to move into that direction (cheap/free apps) because the field is already crowded.

We do, however, need to stay up with digital photography trends. DF4 will support many Sony Alpha cameras, which are becoming very popular, since they take great photos, and since they can capture images without any mechanical shutter or mirror moving around. DF4 will also support some m4/3 cameras for the first time, including the Olympus E-M1/E-M5 II and Panasonic Lumix GH4.

13

Exercise 1

The Traveling Head

Here's an exercise that can be a lot of fun but requires some careful frame-to-frame registration. You will need to have a computer with a program like Dragonframe on it available to work through this exercise. You will also need to have either a digital video camera that feeds into the computer with Dragonframe or a DSLR still camera. The best kind of lens to use is something that is wider than 50 mm. A tripod is critical. You will also need one human subject who is willing to be patient and who has a fair amount of stamina. You can shoot indoors, but this exercise is much more successful if you can execute this outdoors in a variety of environments. If you do shoot outdoors, then it would be best to choose an evenly lit day like an all-sunny day or an evenly overcast day to help reduce an overactive frame due to strong light variations. Shooting in the field has its challenges, and the first challenge you will encounter will be your computer. A laptop computer on battery power will serve for this approach. You can execute this exercise without a computer and just a capture card or flash card in your camera, but the results will not be as tightly controlled. This exercise will help demonstrate the contrast that is required in a pixilated film for it to be viewable and not overly active. The human subject will be the constant and the background will radically change throughout.

Figure 13.1

A human subject lined up head and shoulders in front of an environment.

The idea of this film is to focus frame by frame on your human subject in a head-and-shoulders composition with enough room in the frame around the subject to reveal the environment that your subject is in. The head and shoulders of your subject will travel through different environments as though they are floating through space. The subject can and should react to the different people and situations that he or she travels past by creating fun expressions and actions (Figure 13.1).

Your human subject should stand at a determined distance from the camera that will be mounted on the tripod directly in front of the human with the lens at the eye-level of the human. It would be helpful to have a measuring implement like a ruler to help keep the distance between the lens and the human subject consistent frame to frame.

You are going to travel with your camera and human subject from one location to a second location. You might have the subject start from the front door of the house out to the mailbox, or he or she might travel all the way around the block or go from one side of the city to the other. The distance is up to you. The greater the distance, the more interesting the film can be. If you are traveling long distances, then you could actually use a car to get from one frame position to the next. The key element and critical aspect to watch is the consistent relationship of the camera to the human subject. This is where having a computer with frame-to-frame comparison capability can be very helpful. Holding a laptop and controlling the camera and human placement can be a lot for one person to handle, so you might consider having an assistant that can hold your laptop for you, like a portable table. If you cannot find some

Figure 13.2

An overhead view of the subject defining the constant camera–subject relationship (the length of his arm).

help, then you might not be able to support all those elements, and as a result you might have to judge the placement of your human subject by other means. For example, you can turn on the internal grid in the camera's viewfinder. Another simple means of reference can be to use a string or measuring device to constantly cage the distance between the subject and the camera. I used a 24-mm lens on my camera, and the subject stood exactly an arm's length from the camera. He put out his arm every frame to keep his distance constant, and I centered him up with the viewfinder grid. Your registration and human placement might not be as tight as it would be if you were comparing each new frame with the previous frame for placement with Dragonframe. If you do have a laptop and Dragon, then you might consider using the onion skin option for the most effective human subject placement and registration. I find that shooting one frame per move elicits the best results at 30 FPS but you can try 15 FPS. If you shoot your composition a little wider, then you can push in on your frames in post using After Effects and you can use the tracking/ stabilization feature to line up the eyes frame to frame for a more rock-solid registration (Figure 13.2).

The distance from one position to the next, once you get past the ease-ins, will be determined by how fast you want your subject to travel and how rapidly you want your backgrounds to change. Naturally, the bigger the position change (i.e., 10 feet), the more rapidly your character will travel. Bigger moves are very effective outside because you have large environments. But I recommend that you move your subject about 3 feet. This would work well for going from the house to the mailbox or even around the block, but the longer the distance, the longer your film will be based on a 3-foot move per frame. If the background changes too radically frame to frame, then you might start to lose the effect of forward movement. It's most effective if the background does displace itself at an even rate so we see background elements diminishing in the frame, indicating that we are moving past them (Figure 13.3).

So you will start with your human subject lined up in front of the camera in a still position. I find that it adds a lot to the film if you try to give your human subject some expression of thought or, perhaps, determination. Remember that you

Figure 13.3

Twelve frames of a diminishing background.

have to break down these expressions bit by bit and the extreme or "key" expression should be strong and slightly exaggerated. Your human subject also needs to be able to hold that expression for long periods of time. Be aware of what the eyes are doing. You can begin by just slightly moving your camera on the tripod backwards by about an inch. Move up your human subject to the camera that same inch distance so the relationship of the camera position and human is always consistent. This is the first ease-in movement of your journey.

Remember to ease out your final movements when your human subject comes to rest or is at the end of his or her journey. I also want to remind you to think about controlled animated movements that the human subject might display, like looking left and right frame to frame, smiling, maybe waving a hand, or some other expression that might relate directly to the journey being taken.

The final point I want to relay is that there are endless variations on this exercise. If you refer to Mike Jittlov's *Wizard of Speed and Time*, you will see a wonderful film partly based on this concept and done in a very inventive way. There is one more element that can be added for a more advanced production, and that is the element of blur. If you can find or build a moving unit (it could be the back of a pick-up truck—use extreme caution working in the back of a truck—or a dolly or some sort of rolling platform) that can hold you, your camera and tripod setup and laptop, *and* your human subject, then you can get the blur you need. Your camera and human subject will always be lined up with the proper distance to each other on the moving platform—you won't have to constantly monitor that relationship and you can move them both together by moving the moving platform. In order to get blur, which might be very effective if your character is supposed to be racing through an environment, you need to have a longer shutter exposure, like 1 second. This may require that you stop down the camera lens to *f/22* if you are shooting outside. You can also use ND filters to knock down the exposure. You will need someone to concentrate on moving the platform with you and your subject on it as you shoot the camera. You can adjust your human subject, and on a coordinated count you need to move your platform and simultaneously shoot the camera shutter at one second. Your subject will stay in focus, because it will move exactly the same distance and way the camera moves (since they are on the platform together), but the background will blur because the relationship of the camera and background has shifted during the 1-second exposure. This takes some practice and careful control, but it can be very effective. It's even more important to give some life to your character with this effect so it feels like he or she is active and full of energy, racing through the scene.

If you want to shoot a night scene, you can use a flash-pop or a quick on-and-off light on your subject while keeping your shutter open for a longer period of time, so any moving background elements can blur. It would take a little testing to get the right exposures, but this technique could elicit some really exciting results.

14

Exercise 2
Rotating Human Subjects

This exercise is best when you have the availability of many people. It can be used as a workshop or class event. You will need a single-frame camera like a digital video camera or a DSLR still camera with a 35-mm lens. A tripod is absolutely essential to mount your camera on. It is also important to tape down and bag your camera and tripod because your human subjects may get close to the camera and potentially bump the tripod, ruining your shoot. There are all sorts of variations on this concept. I will run you through one approach, and then you can take the idea and expand on it. Once again, having a computer near and connected to your camera that is equipped with a capture software program like Dragonframe will make a huge difference in the success of this exercise. You will be frame-referencing the position of one human subject to the next, so having onion skin capability will allow you to be fairly close in your registration from one person to the next. When I practice this exercise, I also use a projector that is connected to my computer, so that the image and frame I am working on can be viewed by all the other participants in the exercise. This basically means that this exercise should be shot in an interior space that is protected by the elements and has a steady light source. As I mentioned earlier, you may expand on this idea and take a variation of this exercise outside and see what results you get there.

Here's the setup: Put a chair in the middle of an open interior space and tape down the chair to the hard floor so it is stable. Don't shoot on a soft surface like a carpet. Put your tripod directly in front of the chair with the camera facing the chair. Set the height of the camera at the eye level of a person of average height who is sitting in the chair. Frame it up so that the person in the chair can only be seen as a head and shoulders shot. It's helpful to have a table behind the camera so you can place and operate the computer, and the table might serve as a platform for your projector (if you have one). Your projector should project on the wall behind the camera so the person in the chair can see what is being filmed as they look straight ahead. This is important so that the person in the chair can see where they line up in the frame in relation to the person who was sitting in the chair in the previous frame.

The number of people involved can be anywhere from 2 to 12. The larger the number the more interesting the result can be. Let's say you have 12 people. Line up five standing people starting on the right of the chair and five on the left side of the chair. They should start just behind the chair, with the rest of the people lined up in a row. The eleventh person will operate the camera and work the registration of the twelfth person in the chair. That eleventh person will sit on the desk with the computer and direct the twelfth person, who should be sitting in the chair. The camera should be focused on the person in the chair and the people along the sides of the chair should just be in on the left and right side of the camera frame (Figure 14.1).

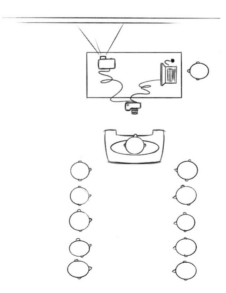

Figure 14.1

An overhead view of the setup.

14. Exercise 2

The reason this exercise is great for a group is because everyone gets to be the central figure in the animation, a peripheral figure, and the animator. This is because everyone has to rotate positions every frame. I like to shoot this exercise at 15 FPS and play back at 15 FPS. That is the same as shooting two frames for every person in the chair if you were shooting at 30 FPS, but the process goes a little faster at 15 FPS.

The rotation proceeds as follows. Once the person in the chair is photographed, he or she carefully gets up and moves to the front of the line that is frame right. Everyone moves back one position on the right-side line and the person at the end of the frame-right line moves over to the back of the frame-left line. The person at the front of the frame-left line goes to the desk to control the camera via the computer. The person who was at the desk shooting the previous frame goes to sit in the chair and so forth (Figure 14.2).

This is another example of how contrasting visual activity and stationary or focused elements in the overall frame direct the viewer's eye. Imagine what the frame will look like with people changing every two frames. It will be highly active, so it becomes very important to find a visual and stable focus for the audience. In this exercise we are animating people, and we have already noted in Chapter 8 that the eyes are a natural visual focus point. So the element that you want to match up in registration (by using the onion skin tool) from person to person is their eyes. When each person sits in the chair, the person behind the

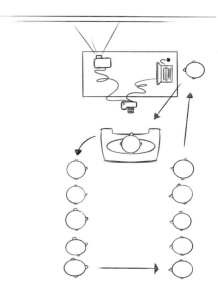

Figure 14.2

Overhead view of the setup with arrows to show the flow of the rotation.

camera working the computer and software should direct the person in the chair to move his or her body around so that the eyes line up as closely as possible with those of the person who was shot in the previous frame. It's best to line up as much of each person's body (head and shoulders) as possible, but the eyes are the main focus. Everybody has a different body shape, so the registration will vary from person to person. If you are using a projector, then the person in the chair can see himself or herself on the screen and get the general lineup of their own body if you project the onion skin image of the live and previous frames. Then the director or animator behind the camera can finesse the position of the person in the chair for closer registration as he or she looks directly into the camera.

Now comes the fun part. As you change out the person in the chair and rotate the group, have your animated subjects think about an action that they want to carry through from person to person. This is especially important for the person in the chair. This action could include changing expressions, blinking eyes, a wave of a hand, or even some lip sync. If you remember from Chapter 3, there is some information about breaking down sound. You can record someone saying something at a rate of 15 FPS, put that on a timeline with a sound wave, and break down that dialog frame by frame on a log sheet. Bring that log sheet to this exercise and the person who is animating or directing the person in the chair can help adjust the mouth of the person in the chair to mimic the words being said. Or just import that recording into Dragonframe and, as you start shooting, line up the poses and actions to the sound wave. The two rows of people behind the chair who are constantly rotating can discuss some kind of action that they want to follow through on, which could include squatting and standing frame to frame, making a wave pattern, or any number of group or individual actions (broken down frame by frame). Remember to use some dynamics in your posed movements so the movement is not just even in its pacing (Figure 14.3).

What you will find in this exercise is that certain things help unify this animated exercise. The constant changing of the people in their positions is too active for the audience to register clearly but the centering and registering of the eyes and mouth (if possible) will help hold the audience's focus. A continuous action, like a wave or having each person position themselves in a sequence of positions for a particular action, will hold the audience's focus and attention, and

Figure 14.3

Several frames of a kissing action in the rotating heads exercise.

that makes this exercise very interesting. One more element that can help unify the moving image is if the person in the chair always wears the same shirt (like a bright red t-shirt). That adds a sense of stability in this highly active sequence.

One really fun example of something similar to this exercise can be seen on YouTube: a study called *Living My Life Faster* by J.K. Keller. It shows an individual shot one frame per day over 8 years and lined up and registered by the eyes (probably with After Effects). The contrast of the locked-in eyes and the rapidly changing elements of clothes and hair make a dynamic and historic account of the evolution of one individual. Although this is one individual and would be categorized as more of a time-lapse exercise, it does give similar results to the exercise you are trying here.

15

Exercise 3
2D/3D Handball

Mixing techniques can result in some very interesting visuals that can be as fun to plan as they are to produce. There are many artists who combine approaches successfully, and it gives their work a unique art direction. One artist we mentioned in previous chapters is the Italian graffiti artist Blu. This stop-motion artist paints graphic 2D images on exterior and interior walls in sequences while shooting a frame-by-frame camera that is in constant motion. Blu also paints three-dimensional objects as he animates them moving through his composition. This combination of the three-dimensional world and the two-dimensional graphic world is seamlessly blended in an organic and practical manner all directly in front of the camera.

Our next exercise will play with this approach. Keep in mind that this exercise can be expanded into an infinite variety of approaches, and I would encourage you to try something of your own design once you have gone through this simple process. As always, you will need a DSLR camera or digital video camera and a tripod to mount the camera on. If you want to incorporate camera moves (which is not necessary), then you may want to add a Manfrotto geared head (410 Junior tripod head or 400 Deluxe tripod head). The geared head can be cranked or turned in small increments for pans and tilts, allowing for ease-ins and -outs. I recommend that you keep your camera in a fixed and locked position by taping down or sand-bagging your tripod and tightening all the control knobs on the tripod once you have set your composition. You will also need an assistant to operate the camera or a human subject who will sit in front of the camera and have his or her hands animated. I recommend that you have a computer with Dragonframe or a similar capture software program so you can compare frames for subject placement and replacement registration. You will need to have a table to work on.

We have created a simple bouncing ball sequence. You can rock and roll this sequence by reversing the cycle once it has completed its forward movement, so the ball appears to bounce up and down and back and forth (once we start moving the cards in the exercise). So you will shoot Cards 1, 2, 3, 4, 5, 6, 7, 6, 5, 4, 3, 2, 1, 2, 3, and so on (Figures 15.1 and 15.2).

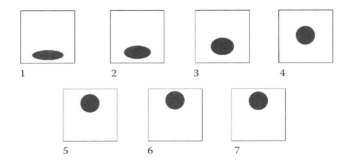

Figure 15.1

The sequence of a 2D bouncing ball cycle.

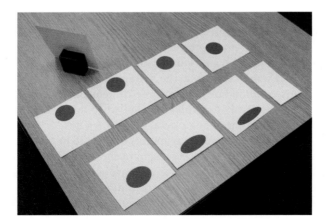

Figure 15.2

The cards laid on a table, with the backing block.

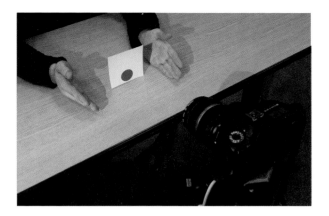

Figure 15.3

The composition of the handball exercise.

You should be able to take this page and put in on a copying machine or scan it and then blow up the sequence so that each frame of the bouncing ball is 4 × 4 inch. Print this series out on card stock, which is a bit heavier than normal paper. You will have a series of seven ball drawings, with one ball on each 4-inch piece of card. You will need a small block of wood or some sort of simple support with a piece of tape or wax to help support each drawing as you replace them in front of the camera for this exercise. You will be bouncing the graphic ball back and forth between your hands as they slowly come together to squash the ball. You should have a simple and clean tabletop that you can sit behind so the camera can point directly at you. It will be much easier if you have an assistant or someone else in front of the camera as you operate the computer and change out the drawings (Figure 15.3).

As the animated subject sits at the table across from the camera, place the hands of the subject together (Figure 15.4).

You will be opening the hands to about 15 inches apart from each other in seven moves and revealing the ball cards between the hands. You will need to have one blank card that is only 2 inches wide as an in-between to reveal the cards. This exercise should be shot at 15 FPS.

You should always start with a 10-frame hold and then slightly part your hands (a quarter to half inch) for an ease-in for the first move. The hands should move apart more on the next frame, allowing the animator to put the 2-inch wide card between the hands (Figure 15.5).

On the third frame, move the hands apart so you can place the first full 4-inch ball cycle card between them and start the replacement ball/card cycle going frame right. Continue to move your hands apart to complete the seven-move sequence until they are about 15 inches from each other. Make sure to ease out from the movement. Each card should be attached to the small support stand

Figure 15.4

The opening position for the exercise (hands together) from the camera point of view.

Figure 15.5

A shot of the hands starting to ease in to their movement apart with a 2-inch card between the hands.

that sits behind the card to hold it upright and should be replaced every frame. The cards and hidden stand should be shifted frame right for each replacement until the card comes up against the frame right hand. That hand should slightly anticipate the ball's arrival by slightly shifting away from the ball as if getting ready to hit the card with the ball on it. The hand will then move about an inch or two forward (frame left) in one frame and then stop and hold, appearing to hit the ball. The ball and card direction and replacement lineup should be reversed and they should start moving frame left. The overall effect is that the hands are bouncing the ball on the cards back and forth (Figure 15.6).

Figure 15.6

The middle position of the animation.

Figure 15.7

The final shot of the hands, far enough apart to reveal the final dimensional ball.

Each time a hand hits the ball card, it should move closer to the other hand as if to squash the ball and card. As a matter of fact, that is exactly what you will do. This merging of the hands on a frame-by-frame basis can happen fairly fast (perhaps over 40 frames). When the hands get close to touching the card on either side, close the hands completely in one move (removing the card completely) and hold the closed hands with no card for about eight frames. Open the hands and reveal a dimensional red ball (if you can find one) or any other object that you want. When you open the hands, include one ease-in movement, slightly revealing the ball or object of your choice; shoot a frame and then open the hands enough to see the ball or object in full. Hold the hands and object for 10 frames (Figure 15.7).

You have successfully mixed techniques all in front of the camera and have practiced some of the "trick" techniques that the early filmmakers like Melies used. Two other great references for this mixing of techniques are the film "Door" by the English artist and director David Anderson and the American independent filmmaker David Russo's film "Pan with Us." The mixture of 2D and 3D elements is explored with models, objects, and photographic sequences shot frame by frame in front of the camera in a fascinating blend of imagery that is both unique and poetic. Once you start to think about the principles here, it should become apparent that there is a vast area to explore in this approach to frame-by-frame filmmaking.

16

Exercise 4
Animated Starburst Light Loop

This frame-by-frame exercise and technique is very popular in Japan. The Japanese refer to it as *pika pika*. They also call it a "lightning doodle project," and often large numbers of people get together to create wonderful, fresh, and vibrant images of light painting in front of the camera frame by frame. So I would like to dedicate this exercise to the people of Japan for their great sense of unity, community, and creativity.

This particular exercise requires a few small props, a dark room or environment, and a DSLR camera like a Canon 5D or a Nikon D-7000. It's important to have one of these digital still cameras because you have a lot of control over the iris, focus, and, most importantly, the shutter speed. The shutter speed of the camera is the critical element in this process. As we saw in previous chapters, the longer the shutter speed, the more you can "smear" images and make moving objects leave a trail of light and color behind them. This is how *pika pika* works. The camera cannot be handheld or have the possibility of being bumped during this process, because your whole image will be smeared and impossible to read. A tripod is, once again, the anchor to making this exercise work. The use of a cable release or a self-timer from the camera's options might be worth considering. Touching the camera to release the shutter risks a slight movement of the camera during the shooting, and the possibility of smearing the whole image is increased. This is why a remote cable or 2-second shutter time-release option is absolutely critical. If you are confident and have a delicate touch, then maybe you can take this risk, but I warn against this approach.

When you shoot an animated light loop, you have to keep in mind that the registration of one frame to the next is difficult to control because there are no registration guides. Even using a capture software program that has frame-to-frame comparison is impractical, but we will consider the possibility of using it in this exercise. You are virtually drawing in three-dimensional space with only your sense of frame-to-frame placement as your guide. As a result, these light paintings have a very kinetic quality that is similar in appearance to painting or scratching directly on film stock. But there are a few things that you can do to help with your drawing.

Besides the camera equipment and dark space, this exercise requires that the person painting the light wear dark clothes. This person will be slightly apparent in the image, which adds a special quality to this technique, but we are going to minimize the light painter's image in this exercise. Our goal is to have a star rise in the frame and then burst and disappear in exactly 15 moves. The film will then be looped so there is an unending rise of stars that burst apart. You want to make sure that the looping has a fun and appealing quality that can be seen over and over again. Let's go back to Chapter 3 and use the star guide that was illustrated in that light-painting description. This guide will help keep the star imagery consistent for the first several frames of the exercise (Figure 16.1).

The star guide should be stabilized and placed very carefully in each frame as it rises into the composition. This will be extremely difficult if you hold the guide by hand with the long camera exposure, so we will use a stand such as a C-stand to hold the star guide. The stand should be "blacked out" by putting black gaffer's tape on it. The C-stand should also be moved to a different position every frame so

Figure 16.1

The star guide with gelled LED flashlights.

Figure 16.2

The C-stand, blacked out with tape, holding the star guide.

that it cannot be seen over a sequence of frames. This can be carefully orchestrated while continuing to raise the star in the frame (Figure 16.2).

Set up your camera with a wide lens like a 24 mm or 35 mm focal range on your tripod at about shoulder height. Let's say you choose to be in a dark room that's mostly empty. Make sure all lights are off (although you may want to have a working light that you can turn on and off as you shoot). This will allow you to place the stand in the right place between shooting frames. This is when you might use your frame-grabbing and comparison capability from the computer. You can shoot a frame with the working light on to see where the stand and star are in the frame, turn off the working light, and perform and shoot the light painting. Then turn the working light back on to place the stand and star in the next position, compare the new placement with the old working light stand and star placement, turn off the light, perform and shoot the next light painting, and so forth. The working light will have to be off during the shooting. You will only need about eight frames of the rising star before it bursts so that is the only period that you may need the working light setup to measure the placement of the star-stand. If you are using a program like Dragonframe to control and shoot your frames, then you can eliminate the working-light shots from the sequence later in post. This whole process can be done without the frame-comparison capability and with no computer. If you choose to just shoot on a flash card in the camera, then think about other means of tracking the star guide placement. This could be by eye, with tape on the floor, or with markings on your stand to guide it as it rises into frame. The problem with the computer is that it emits light in the dark, which can reveal more than you want. This can be resolved by putting a cloth over the screen for each exposure. Programs like Dragonframe have a black-out feature that darkens the screen during the exposure. I leave this option up to you.

When you place the star on the stand in each position for each frame, then you need to light paint. You must have a light source, and that should be a small LED flashlight. You can add or tape a colored gel on the front of the flashlight if you want to have color. There are small LED lights that have color built into them and that might be your best choice for colored light. Each time the shutter is open for the exposure, you need to quickly and precisely (as you can) trace the outline of the star from behind the star, allowing for some of the light to spill over and shine into the camera. It is worth practicing this a few times to see how long it takes to trace out the star. That time should be your ultimate exposure shutter time. You need to take some practice shots to find the proper settings for your camera and to make sure you have the right overall exposure for the light. I should say that this exercise is best executed by two people, although you could do it yourself by using the self-timer option on your camera or a wireless remote. Your shutter speed should end up being somewhere between 3 and 5 seconds long with an adjusted aperture to compensate for the long exposure.

Once the star has hit its zenith in the frame, then you need to remove the stand and star from the frame for the next shot, which will be the beginning of the burst. You will need to have a memory of where in space the star was in its last position (if you are not using a frame grabber). When you are ready to shoot the beginning of the starburst, think about how the light from your LED flashlight should disperse and work from that central point of the star's last placement. The first explosion could be a bright powerful beam that you point directly at the camera and then the sequential frames will be the dispersing light trails. You could use different colored lights for a fireworks effect as the lights get farther out in the composition for each shot (Figure 16.3).

This burst can happen over five or six frames, and each sequential frame of the burst should be more spread out from the last position and smaller in size (Figure 16.4).

Try to finish your small light spots for the end of the burst around Frame 14. That way you have one black frame to complete the 15-frame loop. If you have used Dragonframe, then make a QuickTime movie of the sequence at 15 FPS.

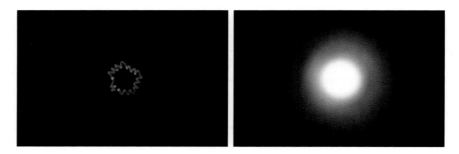

Figure 16.3

An example of options for the beginning of the burst.

Figure 16.4

An image from the end of the burst.

Figure 16.5

Five different key positions for the animated starburst light loop.

Once you have this, you may have to remove the working light frames to show only the light-painted frames. Set the QuickTime to loop and there is your animated light loop. If you are just using a flash card with no frame grabber, then download your files onto a computer. You can place them in a folder and import them into Final Cut by setting the Still/Freeze Duration in Final Cut // User Preferences // Editing to 00:00:00:01. You can also put the frames in an image sequence if you have QuickTime Pro. Make your loop once you have exported to a self-contained QuickTime movie (Figure 16.5).

17

Exercise 5
Dropping Heads (Cutout)

This exercise will require a little photography, some X-Acto knife work, and a simple downshooter setup. It will not be necessary to shoot these cutouts on a downshooter or a piece of glass, but that may add another element for the more advanced animator. You are going to photograph a person (yourself) and then print out that photograph on thin card stock that you can run through a printer. You will then cut out the parts of your body in sections so they can be animated. You will also need a few images from the web and/or magazines with images of different heads that you can cut out and substitute for your own head in the animation. Make sure that these head images are basically in the same scale as your body, although varying the scale a bit can add a lot of humor to this exercise.

Here's how it works. First, take your DSLR camera and set it up on a tripod with a wide lens such as a 35 mm or 24 mm focal length. Have the camera facing a blank wall with no detail on it. Frame it so you can stand in front of the camera (using the self-timer) and shoot a shot of yourself that includes your head down to your knees. Stretch your arms out away from your body, because they will be cut out separately in the cutting phase (Figure 17.1).

You can take several shots with different expressions on your face or even a four-increment head turn of yourself, standing in the same position. You can

Figure 17.1

A shot of the camera setup for photographing the subject (yourself).

add these additional head positions to the animation using the heads as replacements if you want to add a little more dynamic range to your animation exercise, but this is not necessary. Once you have your shot or shots, download them onto a computer and print them out onto thin card stock that you can use in your printer. You should size your images so they can be printed out on an 8.5 × 11 inch piece of paper or card stock.

Take those color printouts of your self-portrait shot and place them on a cutting surface, like a rubber cutting mat. Since you shot your image in front of a blank background, it should be very easy to see and cut out your contour. It is best to use an X-Acto knife to cut out your image from the background. You can use scissors, but they need to be smaller and very sharp to get good clean edges. The next step is to cut apart the image of yourself in several areas. You will want to separate the head from the shoulders. One way to make this cut is to separate the head from the torso at the neckline where your neck goes into the collar of your clothes. The arms should be separated at the shoulders, and the arms need to be cut at the elbows and wrist. Wherever you want to have movement is where you need to make the cut. When you reassemble the parts, remember that there must be a slight overlap of the sections, so your new cutout portrait may be a little shorter than you are. If you print out two copies of your portrait, you can cut the torso out of one copy, leaving the shoulder areas a little longer. Then cut out the arms from the second copy. This way you'll have a little overlap, at least from the shoulder to the upper arm (Figure 17.2).

The next step is where you can have some fun. You are going to animate your character throwing off your head and new heads will appear. So you need to find some different heads that you can photograph yourself, cut out of a magazine, or even find on the Internet and print out. The heads could come from Hollywood stars, politicians, your friends, drawings that you create, insects, or any variety of different heads that you choose. They can vary in scale as long as they have a visual fit to your original body that is believable (Figure 17.3).

Figure 17.2

A layout of the cut parts of the self-portrait body with cutting mat and X-Acto knife.

Figure 17.3

A series of heads that will go on your cutout self-portrait.

These images may be printed on thin paper, so they may require that you give them some backing. I would recommend getting some spray glue and attaching these magazine heads to the thin card stock that you used for printing your own self-portrait. The image can be loosely cut out of a magazine and then attached to the card. Once they are bonded, you can do the careful cutting with the X-Acto knife required to pull the head image from the background.

Now that you have all of your cutout elements, you are ready to set up the camera and shooting area. If you have a downshooter available or have created a setup with a suspended piece of glass and a lower-level background, then place a bright green (ideally a chroma key green) card on that lower level. This way, when you shoot your animation, you can put in any background that you desire later in post. Please refer to Chapter 10 for more information regarding this technique. I want to make sure that this exercise can be simply executed so I will continue as though you do not have a downshooter available. You can shoot these cutouts on a stable, simple, plain tabletop that allows the cutouts to stand out visually. You will also need to get a hold of some beeswax, Blu-tack, or thin double-sided tape (this has the sticky material on both sides of the tape). I recommend using sticky wax, which is often found at miniature and craft stores for holding small objects on shelves. You will use this wax to stabilize your cutout parts as you move them on the tabletop. Assemble your self-portrait together with the cutout parts on the tabletop. Then take your DSLR camera, which should be mounted on your tripod, and raise the tripod pretty high up so you can tilt the head and camera down at the cutout on the table. It is ideal to have the angle of the camera perpendicular to the tabletop, but this is not always possible. One way to allow this to happen is if you can slightly tilt the table up toward the camera. Another technique that you can use is to shoot on a clean floor space with the tripod directly above the cutout shooting area. It is important to note that you will probably have to change the focal length of the lens to something longer, like a 55 mm or even an 85 mm. If you are shooting on the floor and using a zoom lens, then adjust the focal length so you don't see the legs of the tripod but only the cutout model with some room around it. It would be smart to adjust your iris to $f/8$ or smaller (i.e., $f/16$) to help maintain a good depth of field. You will have to connect your camera to a computer that is running Dragonframe or a similar program. Having the frame comparison option to complete this exercise properly will make all the difference (Figures 17.4 and 17.5).

Now you are ready to shoot. You should always start with a hold. This can be 10 frames. I would recommend shooting this exercise at 15 FPS. The idea is to start with your image including all the cut sections with the arms down to the side. If you had replacement heads of yourself turning or making an expression, this would be a good time to substitute those heads. Shoot one frame per head, turn, and hold the extreme head position for at least eight frames. Then turn the head back to the camera. Raise the arms so they are placed as though they are holding the head. Remember your eases and increased increments to get to this position. Hold the arm parts in this head-holding position for eight

Figure 17.4

An example of the tripod pointing down to a tabletop.

Figure 17.5

The composition of the final cutout from the camera point of view.

Figure 17.6

A sequence of cutout frames of the subject changing head parts.

frames, and then have a one-frame ease-in of the hands with the head between the hands separating the head from the shoulders. Then raise the arms and hands up above the body as far as you can, with the head starting to rise just above the hands and being jettisoned out of the upper frame (Figure 17.6).

Once your head is out of frame, bring the arms back down to the sides of the body, matching the opening position. You can refer to the opening frame and make an onion skin comparison with that frame and your final, settled, new position of the arms down to the sides of the body. Once the arms are settled, drop in one of your magazine heads from the upper frame. Have it drop pretty fast (about three to five frames) and settle on your headless body. It would be fun to drop your body down about an inch, ease out, and then raise the body back up to its beginning default position. The end of the arms (hands) should stay in the same position, but keep the shoulder attachment connected to the body so the arms will slightly drop down with the body at the shoulders when the body sinks. This will give the new head a bit of weight when it hits the torso. Once the new head is on, hold for 20–30 frames so we see what the new head is, then raise the arms again to jettison off the new head the same way you did with your original head.

You can carry on this way with as many heads as you like. The final head should be your own head dropping into frame once again. Settle out this final position and compare the body, arms, and head to the original first frame to make it as close in position as possible. This way you can loop your dropping head exercise.

18

Exercise 6

3-2-1 Countdown

This next exercise takes inspiration from frame-by-frame artists like PES. We will use objects and visually create an opening countdown for your films and other visual mediums. Traditionally, these countdowns were used to help sync up a sound track and picture, but they have become part of the filmic language that we know. Each number on a countdown (which can start at 10) should represent a full second, including any movement and the number itself. In our countdown, we will go with the National Television System Committee (NTSC) video frame count of 30 FPS. This will give us enough frames to animate any object we choose on single-frame shots and enough time to see the actual number on a hold of 10 frames (or a third of a second). For the sake of ease and simplicity, we will start our countdown at 3. You certainly can expand on this exercise, as with all of these exercises, and start at 10 with various objects or even people. You might consider using one person for each second of a countdown and having them swing their arm around in a large circle like the second hand on a clock frame by frame, changing the person every 30 frames. That would be another exercise and would require many people and a lot of coordination.

I have decided to execute this 3-2-1 countdown with some everyday objects that I have around the house. I did go digging into my childhood trunk and resurrected my old bag of marbles. I also collect coins from various countries, so some of those Polish and British coins were pulled into service. Finally, I got hungry while searching for the first objects, so I decided to make a bag of popcorn. Eureka—there was my final choice for an interesting object or objects to animate in the countdown. I decided to shoot these objects on a table. You will need a DSLR camera on a taped-down tripod and any lens that gives you enough range or tabletop area to work in. I used a 24-mm lens. I also added a very simple direct light with the barn doors pulled together so it formed two diagonal shadows above and below the numbers (Figure 18.1).

If you can make your animation production time more efficient in the planning stage, then I would encourage you to consider it. For example, once I started working with the marbles on a tabletop I realized that it was going to take me a fair amount of time to make the number 3 with the marbles. Those marbles seemed to have a mind of their own and wanted to roll out of place when I just looked at them, let alone breathed on them. I felt it was going to make my animation very difficult animating forward and trying to get the marbles to fall into place and form a nice, graphic number 3. So I decided to work backwards. This is what I encourage you to do with this exercise. Now, you may not choose to use marbles in your countdown, but whatever you use will look better if you have plenty of time to set up and form the numbers with those objects without having to reach the perfect placement in a straight-ahead forward piece of animation. You can set up the number and get it perfectly placed in the frame so it reads and looks great. If you need a reference, then import an image of the number into Dragon and use the rotoscope feature to line up your objects.

Figure 18.1

The camera, light, and object set up for the 3-2-1 countdown.

Because I decided to work in reverse I first started with the number 1, because that would be at the end of my reverse playback. The number 1 would be formed by my coin collection. I set up the coins to make a number 1, shot 10 frames, and then started my animation. Coins are often stacked, so that is how I animated the individual coins. They collected on top of each other in one column and then the column diminished and disappeared (Figure 18.2).

The popcorn came next. (I was starting to eat the popcorn, so I thought I had better use it before it all disappeared.) Without moving the camera or light, I carefully formed a number 2 with the popcorn kernels. I was shooting on a white background so the popcorn, which is light in value, stood out enough because of the shadows from my key light. Once the number 2 was set up, I shot 10 frames and decided on the best and most interesting way to introduce the corn from the blank frame that would be left after the number 3 popped off. Popcorn pops and explodes, so I decided to randomly pop the corn in a three-object replacement series. This series was a small corn seed for one frame, two or three large popped kernels grouped together for one frame, and then the final replacement was one normal kernel of popped corn (Figure 18.3).

The popcorn would disappear after it popped onto screen when viewed playing forward. Eventually, the popcorn would only pop where the number 2 would be created, and the corn kernels would remain on the table, forming the final number 2 for 10 frames (Figure 18.4).

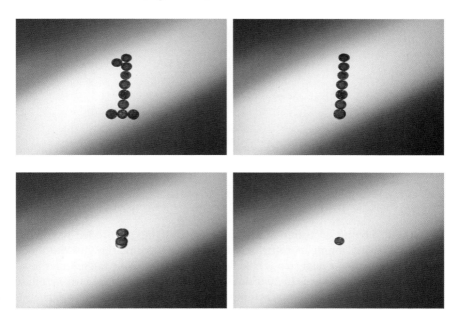

Figure 18.2

The number 1 coin sequence in key positions.

Figure 18.3

A series of popcorn replacements.

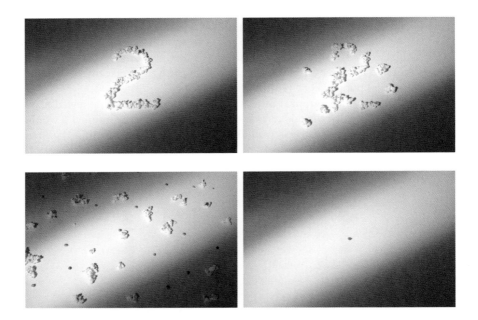

Figure 18.4

The key positions for the number 2 popcorn kernel sequence.

Without moving or bumping the camera and light, I proceeded to my last number. The final number in the countdown was 3, formed by my childhood marble collection The next step was to figure out how to move the marbles in an interesting way (backwards in 20 frames) to form the number 3. Marbles roll, so I wanted to add a little dynamic action to a rolling pattern and have it appear as though the marbles rolled in, squeezed together in a pile, and then burst out into the number 3 for a 10-frame hold (Figure 18.5).

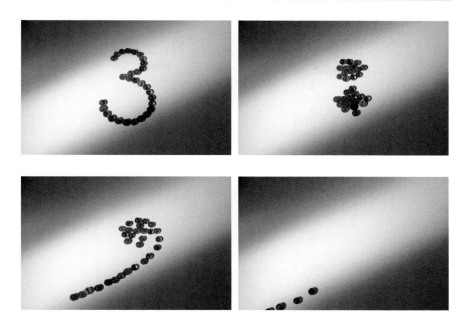

Figure 18.5

A series of key positions for the marbles forming the number 3.

Once all the numbers were shot and the animation was complete, I cleaned up the tabletop and proceeded to edit. Because the camera and light remained in the exact same position, I had all sorts of freedom in the edit area. As I mentioned earlier, I decided to shoot backwards but I wanted the action to move forward, and so I had to apply a reverse playback to the footage to see my final effect. You can view a reverse playback in Dragon, but you will need to export your frames to Final Cut or After Effects to kick out a reverse playback QuickTime movie. Your final results will be the marbles rolling on to form the number 3 for 10 frames, then a blank frame gets invaded by popping corn kernels, ultimately forming a number 2 for 10 frames, and finally a stack of coins grows and disperses into the number 1. On the end of the exact 3-second count, the animated countdown will be complete. There are all sorts of combinations and possibilities for animating a countdown, and this exercise will hopefully spark some ideas of your own that you can expand upon. For inspiration you can view the 1987 film *Academy Leader Variations*, directed by Jane Aaron and Skip Battaglia.

19

Exercise 7
Love at First Sight

This final exercise combines several different elements that we have explored in this book. It has a camera move, human pixilation, downshooting elements, and some composite work. One more challenge that I have incorporated in this exercise is the requirement to shoot outside. Not only will you shoot outside but it will also be important to shoot each frame at an even interval so that any shadow and light play throughout the composition will move in an even fashion. The inspiration for this exercise comes from the great designer and animator Tex Avery.

The camera will approach a young man sitting on a bench outside. The subject looks left and right (in pixilation) and suddenly stops turning and looks directly at someone offscreen. The camera cuts to a close-up of a girl batting her eyes at the young man. The film cuts back to a close-up of the young man. He blinks his eyes, and vibrating paper hearts grow out of his eyes. His ears blow steam (cotton) and then the young man starts to get up, heading frame left. The couple glide together and spin around each other and glide away from the camera into the sunset, leaving a trail of hearts (if you can time this right).

I recommend that you shoot the pixilation of the couple first and then go into the studio and create and shoot the hearts and cotton steam on a down-shooter with a green screen. For the exterior pixilation work, you will need a

Figure 19.1

The setup for the man on the bench and the camera on a tripod.

DSLR camera on a tripod with a 24-mm lens. The wider lens will give the shot a sense of drama. This is another situation where it would be nice to have a laptop with a program like Dragonframe or Stop Motion Pro for capturing the frames and for frame comparison and registration. Having an assistant that carries the laptop will make your life easier. If you cannot get a hold of a laptop, then you will have to shoot on a flash card and use practical means of registration like you did in the Traveling Head exercise (Exercise 1). This means lining up your subject through the viewfinder. Remember that some cameras have a grid-focusing screen for the viewfinder, if this will help you register your subject. This is not a necessary component to help you locate your subject within the frame (Figure 19.1).

Line up your young man on the bench with your camera and shoot a 30-frame hold. Pick up your camera and tripod and ever so slightly move them forward toward the man on the bench. You are easing in on the move toward your subject. Increase your moves forward while trying to keep your subject centered in the frame. You should shoot at 30 FPS because camera moves are always best shot on single frames. This will take some of the strobing out of the move and make it smoother. Remember to ease out your camera move as you approach your subject, keeping him lined up in the center of the frame. It might be best to frame up your subject first for composition before you start shooting and then move your camera back to find the beginning position. This way, you'll know exactly where you're going before you start (Figure 19.2).

Have your young man look frame left and then frame right. Don't rush this movement, allowing about 2 seconds for each direction. You can shoot two frames for every movement at this point. Finally, have your subject look slightly to the left of center frame and try to animate him doing a double-take. This will incorporate a head bob and some blinking. On a second blink hold his eyes open for 20 frames. This is where you will composite the hearts in later. Then have him blink again (wiping away the hearts). Continue to hold this position for an additional 2 seconds. This is the place that you will composite in the cotton steam in post.

You must then get a close-up shot of the girl. The girl should be onscreen for about 3 seconds. She can look rather coy and blink several times. Remember to keep the action exaggerated for the dramatic effect (Figure 19.3).

Figure 19.2

The composition of the close-up of the young man on the bench.

Figure 19.3

The close-up shot of the girl.

Cut back to the same close-up of the young man. He should smile and then start to get up from the bench. This should be animated at the end of the first shot and can be edited later on. The next shot will be a wide shot of the boy approaching the girl. He can slide on one foot (after all, he's in love). Frame-by-frame walking will take too long and will break the flow of the piece. They should embrace and start to spin in a circle. This can be an accelerated pace to add a little dynamism to the scene. You could try having the couple lift their feet off the ground by jumping during the camera exposure when they are in the accelerated spin. This spin is an area to be creative and have fun (Figure 19.4).

Finally, the couple should quickly stop the spin, holding hands side by side. They will each lift one foot and glide away from the camera and toward the sunset (if you have planned your shoot at the right time of day and in the right weather conditions—a sunny day). A trail of hearts will be left behind as they recede into the distance. These can be the same hearts that you used for the young man's eyes. It is important to remember that each exposure should be shot at an even interval of time so the shadows and light will move evenly throughout each shot. You can achieve this by putting your camera on a time-lapse setting and using a remote cable with a time-lapse option or if you are using a connected laptop with capture software. I would guess that an interval of about 30 seconds would give you enough time to arrange everything between shots (Figure 19.5).

Now it's time to head to the downshooting stand. If you don't have a stand, then all you need is a piece of glass and a sheet of green-screen material. You must find a way to mount the glass at a distance from the green-screen board and light them both evenly. You should have a series of five hearts that grow from nothing.

Figure 19.4

An example of the wide shot of the couple and the spin.

Figure 19.5

The final composition of the couple gliding away.

19. Exercise 7

These can be cut out from red paper. The fourth heart will be your main heart. The fifth heart will be bigger than your main number four heart, and you will get a slight stretch and squash effect by using this sequence. So your shooting sequence will be Hearts 1, 2, 3, 5, 4 (Figure 19.6).

Shoot the hearts once on the stand from nothing to Heart 1, 2, 3, 5, 4. Hold heart number 4 and slightly move it to give it a subtle vibration for 20 frames.

The next step is to take some cotton (cotton balls from the drug store will work) and fabricate a series of five growing cone-shaped cotton puffs of steam (Figure 19.7).

This series gets shot once starting with cotton puffs 1, 2, 3, 4, and finally 5. Hold on cotton puff 5 for 20 frames, slightly moving it frame by frame so it vibrates. Try to keep the cotton from having too many see-through areas so it doesn't become too difficult to pull off the green screen in post. You should consider using a de-spill filter in After Effects when you pull the cotton off the green-screen background. You can also change the cotton color option to black and white to get rid of any green spill on the cotton edges.

Figure 19.6

The series of cutout paper hearts.

Figure 19.7

A series of cotton replacements that will serve as steam shooting out of the young man's ears.

Figure 19.8

Two shots side by side of the composited hearts and cotton steam effect.

Now you are ready to go into composite and edit. The first step is to remove the hearts and the cotton steam puffs from the green-screen backgrounds. For the sake of brevity I will refer you to Chapter 10 in the exercise that Jeff Sias described with the flying saucer in After Effects. You need to get the hearts and the cotton steam onto an alpha channel so they can be matched up and scaled to the pixilation footage. Placing the hearts in the young man's eyes will require some placement transforming (moving the heart around in the close-up shot of the young man), scaling, and possibly some color correction or opacity adjustments. Once the young man opens his eyes, then start the growing heart. When he closes his eyes, you can reduce the heart series quickly, making sure that the heart looks like it stays behind the eyelid. Then as the young man continues to look offscreen in that first shot, start the cotton steam effect and let it cycle in the vibration mode. Reverse the cotton growth, and then it's time to cut to the close-up of the girl. You might reduce the opacity of the cotton layer to help make it look a little more like steam (Figure 19.8).

Once this is complete, you need to go to the final shot of the couple gliding away. This is where a trail of hearts is left behind them as they exit from the camera. These hearts can be the same cycle that you used in the eyes repeated randomly around the frame. They can be scaled and duplicated five or six times. Each heart can grow on, and then you can either reverse the growth at the end or dissolve the heart off. This can be done in After Effects or even Photoshop on a frame-by-frame basis.

If the camera move at the beginning is too rough for your taste, then you may apply some stabilizing tracking by slightly blowing up the frames and finding some tracking points to lock onto to smooth out the track in. Once this is complete, then the shots need to be exported from After Effects and brought into Final Cut or a comparable editing program. Make your edits (cutting on the action of the young man getting up from the bench). You might consider a fade up in the beginning and a fade out at the end. There are many variations that you can make to this exercise, and it is just a kicking-off spot for you to consider when trying to mix and match techniques in a unified film. Have fun with *Love at First Sight*!

20

Exercise 8

Cycles

These days, there are so many venues for animated cycles. You can put them on your phone, on your website (as animated GIFs), or as screen savers. The one thing I like about animated cycles is that they give the filmmaker a manageable amount of animation, which can be carefully crafted (or not), so that the novice or experienced animator can accomplish some fun animation in a short period of time. We have seen several animated cycles in this book, from the candy corn from PES to the animated light loops in Exercise 4. The key to cycles is that it is important that the first and last frame have a compositional relationship with each other so that the last frame can sequence right into the first frame without any interruption or misregistration.

In the tradition of the old "trick films," the first exercise I want to share is the spinning head cycle. This is a simple exercise that is best done with Dragonframe or a similar capture software program. There are a couple of key spots where the frame comparison mode is critical. You will need your DSLR camera with a 35-mm lens (or a lens close to that range) and a tripod. Set them up and hook up the camera to Dragonframe. Create a new project. For props, you will need a simple stool and a human subject. Sit the person on the stool and compose the shot to only include the head and torso. The person must wear

Figure 20.1

A series of three shots of the setup.

a piece of clothing that has a distinctive front and back over the torso. I chose a sports jacket with an open front. I also chose a hat for the subject to wear with a distinctive front (like a baseball cap). Basically, you will be creating a 12-frame cycle of the human subject turning around 360 degrees, but the hat and jacket will remain facing toward the camera in each frame, so the person looks like they are turning around inside their clothes (Figure 20.1).

There are no "holds" on cycles, so you start right in on the animation. For the first several frames, the subject will turn his or her head in a clockwise manner. Take the hat off for each slight turn of the head and put it back down on the head facing forward as it did in the first frame. Eventually, your subject will not be able to turn his or her head any more (due to human limitations). At this point the subject must carefully get off the stool, take the jacket off, and put it back on backwards. Have the subject sit back down on the stool and use your onion skin or frame flip-flop comparison to get the jacket to look as close to the way it did in the previous frame, lining up the opening of the jacket. Have the subject turn his or her head counterclockwise to find the next position for the head in a full 360-degree turn. Don't forget to arrange the hat so it is facing forward (no matter how awkwardly it sits on the subject's head). For the next six frames, the subject will turn his or her head clockwise in even increments (always adjusting the hat). When the subject can no longer turn his or her head, have him or her get off the stool and put the jacket on correctly, matching it up to the previous frame as best as possible. Then adjust the hat and shoot another frame. The subject should look like the first frames but his or her head will be turned screen right. Keep animating the head turn to come close to the first frame. With Dragonframe you can put the cursor on the first frame and hit number 5 to compare it to the live frame. Remember that the last frame should be one full move or increment before the first frame so the film can play in a continuous loop or cycle. This is such a simple and fun exercise, but it does require a few careful lineups of parts, which is the heart of animation (Figure 20.2).

The next cycle exercise will require a looser approach with a smartphone. We were using an iPhone 5S with the Stop Motion Studio app. The phone/camera will be held by hand, not a tripod. As mentioned before, iPhones can be a great

Figure 20.2

A shot of six images in a horizontal sequence, demonstrating the body turn.

Figure 20.3

A wide shot of the water tower.

way to experiment with an animation idea, but the quality will not be as good or stable as a sequence shot on a DSLR camera (Figure 20.3).

    There is a water tower near where I live that has always been a favorite spot for graffiti artists to express themselves. There is some great work on those towers. The towers are large cylindrical forms that go straight into the ground. I turned my smartphone sideways and started to capture frames going around the tower. I estimated the space between the tower and the ground area from frame to frame visually and kept taking shots. Since the composite of the forms is pretty close one frame to the other and only the texture or painting changes, it makes for

Figure 20.4

A man shooting with a smartphone around the tower.

Figure 20.5

A series of three shots of the water-tower sequence.

a perfect cycle. The composition of Frame 1 is the same as my last frame, which was 10. You can shoot almost anything in a cycle if it has this kind of relationship one frame to the next.

I want to mention that you can shoot at any rate (FPS) that you want. This will determine the rate of the playback. I like to shoot at 15 FPS, but 30 works well (Figures 20.4 and 20.5).

21

Exercise 9

The Cartoon Punch

Movement is critical to all animation. How you move a person, object, or model tells everything about that subject. Do you follow or copy from nature directly, or will you try to create your own style of movement? We have stated that exaggeration is important, and that is what is used in some of the great Warner Brothers cartoon animation. So let's try that cartoon style on a human and see how it works.

I call this exercise the "Cartoon Punch" because this is very much in the world of cartoons with fast impact, blur effects, and several other principles of animation. If you want to try this yourself, then know that it is very simple on the setup. Once you see how this works, you may also discover that there are many variations on this animation that keep the exercise in the "cartoon" realm. All you need is a tripod, DSLR camera with a wide-angle lens, and a computer with capture software like Dragonframe. You will need two subjects (people) to animate. I find that the two subjects should be close to the same size, so when the punch hand goes across the face of the second subject it looks like it connects. No one actually gets punched or hurt. You are just creating the illusion of a powerful punch.

Figure 21.1

Camera and animated subject setup for the Cartoon Punch.

Set up the camera with something similar to a 24-mm lens so it is facing a three-quarter view of the two subjects. This will be a wide shot that allows for some big movement. Connect to Dragonframe after creating a new project. Finally, set the camera controls through Dragonframe. You need to set the shutter speed to be a third of a second so there is the potential for blur when there is movement during the exposure. Adjust your iris to accommodate the longer shutter speed. You should also make sure that your playback is in high-resolution mode so you can see the blur frames (Figure 21.1).

I shot at 15 FPS and I started with an eight-frame hold. The puncher needs to "anticipate" the punch with a small wind-up frame by frame. There should be a four-frame hold at the peak of the anticipation set position. The puncher then starts the punch in a few increments with a swing arc. Keep in mind that the puncher must hold steady because of the long shutter exposure. When the punch appears to hit the face of the second subject, then that second person needs to move back in three movements to a wall. The punched subject must stick out their arms and then move (stepping backwards) during the exposure so there is a blur effect (Figure 21.2).

The punched subject should appear to slam up against the wall with an eight-frame hold, then move increment by increment into a slow progressive slide down the wall to a collapsed position on the floor, similar to an exaggerated cartoon take.

Another variation on the Cartoon Punch can be simpler and more direct. It requires the same setup with the same long shutter exposure, but instead of

21. Exercise 9

Figure 21.2

Six frames of the actual punch positions with a blur effect of an "extended punch."

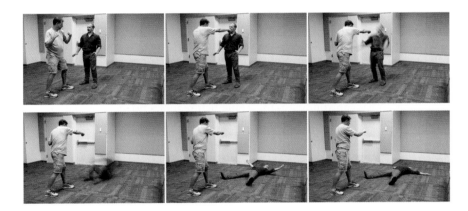

Figure 21.3

A sequence of six frames from the Cartoon Punch (direct).

sliding across the room the punched subject simply falls (carefully) backwards during the exposure, after being punched, in two frames and almost immediately assumes a "flattened" position on the floor. My two subjects were also filmmakers, so they wanted to put some things on the floor, like a woman, a term paper, or a court summons so there would be a suggested story just from the visual environment. You can certainly do this sort of thing, but I am more interested in making sure that the animation and movement are the central focus. One thing that my subjects incorporated was expression. I asked the puncher to look angry and the punched to be surprised. This adds a lot to the fun and interest in the animation and is often something that gets left out with novice pixilated films (Figure 21.3).

Finally, I want you to consider some postproduction editing or manipulation. This kind of frame shuffling has always been a part of trick films from the beginning with artists like Melies. In the first punch exercise, I pulled several frames out of the section where the punched subject slides down the wall. I felt it needed a little more dynamism and speed. I had to be very careful that the frames I pulled from the punched character did not affect the swing and recoil of the puncher. I had the puncher settled into his final general position as the slide was occurring, so the removal of these three frames did not affect the puncher's action.

Another effect that you can try is to freeze or rock and roll the extreme hold positions, like the anticipation of the punch. Again, you must be careful about the freeze effect on the soon-to-be punched subject. Since this is a "locked-off" camera with no camera move, you can also go into After Effects or Photoshop and split up the subjects by dividing the frame in two or rotomatting the characters. This only gets tricky when the two characters overlap each other. If you decide to play around with the timing this way, then make sure that you shoot a clean plate of the environment without the subjects in the frame. You will have proper background information should you need it in the repositioning of the characters.

I have just given you a few basics of cartoon movement through this exercise and I would challenge you to expand upon this basic approach. What can you do to have the subject go straight up out of frame after the punch? What does it look like to give the puncher a swirling, blurry hand as he goes into the windup before the punch? What can you put in the frame that requires no more work but helps tell a story of why the punch is happening? Consider these ideas and more, and have a blast with the Cartoon Punch!

Index

Note: Page numbers in *italics* indicate figures.